"Unparalleled will deepen your understanding and appreciation for the Christian faith—so unique and distinctive."

teach_____ _____ *Fan*; _____ _____ _____ church

"Read this book to shore _____ _____ don't stop there. Share it with s_____ _____ st on who Christians are and w_____

Russell Moore, president, Southern Baptist Ethics & Religious Liberty Commission

"Jared skillfully reminds us that, through Jesus, the Christian faith is sustained by grace and meets our needs at every level."

Caleb Kaltenbach, author of *Messy Grace*; lead pastor of Discovery Church

"Like handling a diamond, Jared turns to the foundational doctrines of the Christian faith, shining light on the edges that come together to make Christianity unique."

Trevin Wax, managing editor of The Gospel Project; author of *Gospel-Centered Teaching, Clear Winter Nights,* and *Counterfeit Gospels*

"Unparalleled is a reliable guide of clear and artfully illustrated truths about Christianity."

Gloria Furman, cross-cultural worker; author of *The Pastor's Wife* and *Missional Motherhood*

"Jared reveals through truth and grace that Christ's way is like no other."

Vince Antonucci, author of *God for the Rest of Us*; lead pastor of VERVE

"With characteristic wit and style, Jared weaves in and out of perplexing doctrines such as the exclusivity of the gospel, the baffling nature of the Trinity, and the uniqueness of Christ."

Jonathan K. Dodson, lead pastor of City Life Church; author of *The Unbelievable Gospel* and *Raised? Finding Jesus by Doubting the Resurrection*

"Unapologetically, the gospel of Jesus is *counter:* counter-intuitive, counter-culture, counter-self, and even counter-religion. And yet, it is its 'counter-ness' that causes the gospel to stand out as not only plausible but wonderfully compelling. Jared Wilson does a magnificent job showing us why."

Scott Sauls, senior pastor of Christ Presbyterian Church, Nashville, Tennessee; author of *Jesus Outside the Lines: A Way Forward for Those Who Are Tired of Taking Sides*

"*Unparalleled* demonstrates why Christianity is the true faith that has no real rivals and is the only hope for lost humans and our broken world."

Nathan A. Finn, dean of the School of Theology and Missions, Union University, Jackson, Tennessee

"Jared Wilson's *Unparalleled* is a stirring reminder of just how different Christianity is from any other faith. Readers will come away emboldened to witness for Christ and encouraged in the grace we have in him."

Thomas S. Kidd, Distinguished Professor of History, Baylor University

"Jared Wilson successfully does what many apologetics and evangelistic books fail to accomplish: he speaks to the deeper existential crises and heart desires of the lost. He offers a guide to the Christian faith marked by courageous clarity and poignant storytelling."

Daniel Montgomery, lead pastor of Sojourn Community Church, Louisville, Kentucky; founder of the Sojourn Network; author of *Faithmapping*, *PROOF*, and *Leadership Mosaic*

"Jared Wilson has written a compelling, attractive, and lively account of what makes Christianity so distinctive."

Sam Allberry, associate minister of St. Mary's Church, Maidenhead, England; author of *Is God Anti-Gay?*

"This book beautifully presents the distinctions of Christianity and implores followers of Jesus to stop making him look so normal. This is a book you should put in the hands of every Christian."

Daniel Darling, author of *The Original Jesus*; vice president of communications, ERLC

"*Unparalleled* is a gospel-drenched adventure into the uniqueness of God. Confessional and winsome, Jared's writing guides us from the foothills of faith to the Himalayas of holiness."

Christian George, assistant professor of historical theology and curator of the Spurgeon Library at Midwestern Seminary; author of *Godology* and *Sex, Sushi, and Salvation*

UNPARALLELED

HOW CHRISTIANITY'S UNIQUENESS
MAKES IT COMPELLING

JARED C. WILSON

BakerBooks

a division of Baker Publishing Group
Grand Rapids, Michigan

© 2016 by Jared C. Wilson

Published by Baker Books
a division of Baker Publishing Group
P.O. Box 6287, Grand Rapids, MI 49516-6287
www.bakerbooks.com

Printed in the United States of America

Library of Congress Cataloging-in-Publication Data is on file at the Library of Congress, Washington, DC.

ISBN 978-0-8010-0859-7

16 17 18 19 20 21 22   7 6 5 4 3 2 1

This book is dedicated to Macy and Grace.
May you treasure the truths of God's Word
and experience his grace always.
I have written this book praying for you most of all,
that you would see the wonder
and the beauty of your faith.

Contents

7

Contents

Acknowledgments

Insights and inspiration from many people have served the writing of this book, but I am compelled to mention at least a few. Chapter 1, the trickiest chapter to write in many ways, would not have developed without many wonderful conversations with my friend Christian George, the curator of Midwestern Seminary's Spurgeon Library. Thank you for your wisdom and encouragement, friend.

This work also leans heavily on the thoughts of great men like Ray Ortlund, Tim Keller, Martin Luther, and C. S. Lewis. Pastor Erik Raymond unlocked a beautiful truth about Romans 3:26 that helped me immensely. I am also very grateful for the field of my former ministry, Middletown Springs Community Church in Vermont—and the beautiful people of New England in general—for providing the space and opportunity to see what the message of Jesus might do in places where it seems so foreign and strange to so many.

My agent, Don Gates, was a valuable coach throughout the composition of the book. The kind folks at Baker Books, including my editor Brian Thomasson, have been enthusiastic cheerleaders of this project from start to finish. But mostly I must thank Becky, who is my best friend and a greater partner in the adventure of grace than I could have dreamed.

Introduction

All I wanted was a haircut.

I hadn't planned on discussing life and death, good and evil, or heaven and hell. But God had other plans. And so did the hairstylist.

It happens to me almost every single time. I sit down in that neat-o hydraulic chair, get that flimsy vinyl apron wrapped around my neck, and the hair starts falling along with the pleasantries. It's not too long into the process until the hairstylist asks the question nearly every man is asked in these shoot-the-breeze type scenarios: "So, what do you do?"

I have a lot of options here, if I want to get creative. I could say, "Nothing, really. I just kind of sit around, mostly." Or I could say, "I ponder the limitless nature of cold, dark

space and our futile place in the dank blackness of it all."
You know, if I'm feeling cheeky.

But I know what's really being asked: "What do you do
for a living?"

She's asking about my job. I have two honest and direct
options to give here. If I want to avoid a religious debate,
if my introversion is really flaring up that day, or if I just
feel too weary of spiritual conversation, I could say, "I'm a
writer." But then I will always be asked about what I write.
And that puts me right back in the position of my most
honest response. So I just say it: "I'm a pastor."

Now, if you're cutting hair in the Bible Belt or some
other religion-thick places in the United States, this may
elicit no more than an arched eyebrow. Where I come
from in the South, you can throw a rock out your window and probably hit a pastor. But where I most recently
lived—in the least churched state in the least churched
region of the nation—there is no way to avoid a serious
conversation about religion. For the average Vermonter,
having a conversation with an evangelical pastor ranks
somewhere between seeing Bigfoot and getting abducted
by aliens.

Okay, it's not that rare. But it's not common.

After I've shared that I'm a pastor, there is usually an
awkward silence. Just for a few seconds. I know the hairstylist is processing the information, trying to determine
the correct response to my unanticipated information.

After she's figured out where I pastor—a very little town
in the county that even many locals aren't too familiar
with—she may ask about the community there or how my

12

kids like the schools. But the conversation usually comes around to this appraisal of my occupation: "That's nice."

And then she says what they all say. If I had a nickel for every time I've heard it, I could . . . well, I could probably afford a haircut. My interviewer almost always offers some variation of "I'm spiritual but not religious."

The literal interpretation of this statement really boils down to this: "I think it's nice you do that, but I'm not really into organized religion."

"I'm spiritual but not religious." I hear it a lot, not just from hairstylists. Lots of people in New England say things like this. And many of them really do subscribe to some kind of amorphous "spirituality." In the little town where I pastored the only evangelical church in the community, there were weekly guided meditation meetings. There are gatherings on Halloween night to summon the spirit of the fire. We had channelers and psychics in our town, mystics and manipulators of crystals. Vermont can be pretty New Agey. Many people are spiritual but not religious.

Truth be told, however, what most people there who say, "I'm spiritual but not religious" really mean is, "I literally never think about anything spiritual or religious until somebody like you brings it up." We live in a true post-evangelical, post-Christendom spiritual wilderness.

And yet here I am, just trying to get my hair cut, and I go and ruin this lady's autopilot chitchat with my very livelihood. On this particular visit to the salon, I was prepared for the question and for the response. Part of me, I'm sad to say, was hoping to avoid the whole thing. I just wanted a haircut! But I was also prepared for God's other plans. Our conversation went pretty much like this:

"I'm spiritual but not religious," she said.

"That's cool," I said. "How would you describe your spirituality?"

"Well, you know, I just try to be a good person. I think if you put positive things out there, positive things will come back to you. There's a lot of negativity in the world."

"Yep. There sure is. Would you say, then, that you think most people in the world are negative?"

"It seems like it. Not everybody. But lots of people."

"But not you?"

"Well, I'm not perfect, of course. But I do try my best to put positive energy into the world."

(A lot of Vermonters are really big on positive energy and the like.)

"So, for you, being spiritual is about doing good things," I said.

"Yeah, pretty much. Just try to be a good person, put more positive energy out there, try not to get too distracted by the negative, and just basically be kind and all that."

It's at this point I am reminded that this is the general outlook of *just about everybody in the history of the universe.* They may all describe it or define it in different ways, but this kind of moral calculus is the basic default setting of every human being, religious or irreligious, who has ever existed. *I just need to be good. I need to be more good than bad. If I do more good things than bad things, I am a good person. And since I am a good person, I can do more good things than bad things.*

There are exceptions, of course, but this is how most people think. This is why many Southerners go to church every Sunday and why many New Englanders don't. Because they're "good people."

I have found, in this largely non-Christian culture, that this kind of conversation leads to an incredible evangelistic entry point. By and large, people in my community have rejected organized religion and all that goes along with it, because they have determined that they can be "good people" just fine without it. And here's the kicker: *they can.*

You can work on your positive energy output, on making sure the good side of your scales bears more weight than the bad side, all without the help of a church or a sacred book or any of the stuff that comes with an actual religion. You can be "spiritual but not religious." And many try it. In my part of Vermont, families who worship no divine being at all teach their children manners; homeschool them; don't let them watch TV; train them to reduce, reuse, and recycle; and all that. They are, as far as trying to be "good" goes, good people. They've figured out they don't need the church to do any of those good things, and they're pretty much right.

So it's my job—and the job of every Christ-following believer everywhere—to do the wonderful job of exploding all this tidiness with the most radical notion these folks have ever heard: *trying to be good isn't the point.*

When I want to share the message of Jesus with someone, I nearly always ask what I then asked my hairstylist that day: "What would you say the message of Christianity is?"

I have literally never heard an unbeliever reply with the message Christians call "the gospel." Never. Their response is always some variation of what they've already said they try to do without the help of a religion: "be a good person."

I don't know if they think the message of Christianity is "be good" because they've never heard the gospel or because the evangelical church has done a terrible job of making the gospel clear. I suspect it's a fair amount of both. In any event, the door is now wide open to correct the misunderstandings, to clear the air, to present the good news.

Make no mistake, in the public marketplace of religious conversation—in the entire world of spiritual, unspiritual, religious, irreligious, theistic, deistic, polytheistic, atheistic, political, moral, liberal, conservative, moderate, or whatever kind of ideas—Christianity is at a great advantage. Why? Because in the midst of this murky multi-ideological fog, Christianity stands alone and above, a solitary lighthouse shining real light. The truth claims of Christianity are unlike those of any other religion, philosophy, or system in the world.

See, the world of "spiritual but not religious" people think all these religions and philosophies are really all the same. Atheists argue that all spiritualities are alike. Universalists claim all sacred roads lead to the same place. Moralists find their legal foundations in all great ancient texts, not to mention in politics and in art. But Christianity is utterly different.

"What if I told you," I said to the lady holding sharp scissors near my head, "that the message of Christianity was that none of us is really good deep down"—I usually add, "including pastors"—"and that we can never be sure our good stuff is greater than our bad stuff, but that God loves us anyway and will consider bad people good?"

This is usually confusing. But intriguing. If no rational person would consider a bad person good, how could God?

"The essential message of Christianity," I said, "is not that we should be religious or try to do lots of good works. The essential message of Christianity is that God loves bad people so much that he sent Jesus to die on the cross to forgive them, so that if anyone stops trusting their own good works and starts trusting Jesus, they will be declared good forever and be saved from judgment."

I will be honest in that I have not seen one hairstylist, including this one, receive Christ as their Lord and Savior through this conversation. But plenty have heard the actual message of the Bible for the very first time.

It is my conviction that as Christians press forward into this brave new world of growing unbelief and skepticism, we must learn what makes Christianity so diffcrent from all the rival philosophics the world thinks all blend to-gether. We will not stand out by first of all "being good." The unbelieving world has learned they can try to do that without our Jesus. Especially since so many of us who follow Jesus can't seem to get the "being good" thing right ourselves.

And a lot of this kind of thinking in the modern world has become more intellectual. The rejections of the Christian faith today are much more sophisticated (and hostile) than they used to be. Christianity is only seen as another variation of a universal set of truths. Cynics and critics argue, in fact, that Christianity's essential truth claims are only repackaged versions of ancient myths and folk stories.

But are they?

It is a well-worn truth that to spot the counterfeit, you must study the real thing. Christians have to get back to the basics of our faith and its implications and really see how different Christianity actually is. The more familiar we get with the truth claims of our faith, the more we see how utterly unique they are. From the Bible's teaching on God himself to Christ's work, from our message to our mission, Christianity is unlike anything else.

I know there are plenty of books on apologetics and worldview that help Christians defend against challenges to the faith. But we can't learn these answers just to win arguments. That is the way everybody else in the world talks religion. Christianity has never made converts primarily by winning arguments but rather by capturing hearts.

What's great about the Christian faith isn't just that it's right but that it's *powerful*. The apostle Paul writes, "We destroy arguments and every lofty opinion raised against the knowledge of God, and take every thought captive to obey Christ" (2 Cor. 10:5). Rightly understood and appropriately shared, what the Bible teaches can dismantle its opponents' objections while captivating their souls.

The basic tenets of biblical Christianity answer the intellect's most nagging questions, and at the same time the heart's deepest longings (Ecc. 3:11; Acts 17:23; Rom. 8:23).

While there are obviously some similarities between the Christian faith and other religions, I want to show you in the chapters ahead how Christianity's utter uniqueness makes it utterly compelling. There really is no other philosophy, message, or way of life like it.

The Great Big Personal God

HOW THE CHRISTIAN GOD
IS NOT LIKE THE OTHERS

"Take terrorism, for example," said our Muslim cab driver.

I confess I got a little tense. Sometimes, before I even know it, I find myself in religious conversations. And sometimes I actually go looking for them. Though I wrestle with it at times, for me this is an important part of what it means to be a Christian. I believe in a personal God who wants people to know him, and I believe he has tasked Christians with the mission of bringing the good news about this personal relationship to other people. If I really love God, I will love my neighbors. And if I really love my neighbors, I will want them to love God. And if I really want them to love God, I will tell them about God.

And this is why, when my friend Jonathan and I were in a taxi cab in Washington, DC, one sunny afternoon, we initiated a religious conversation with our driver. It turned out he was Muslim, but he admitted he didn't go to mosque that often and wasn't a very strict practitioner. Still, he had been raised in the faith by devoted parents and had some very strong beliefs about God—and he did use the word *God*, not *Allah*—that he was eager to share with us.

Over our too-short drive, we discussed the biblical history of the patriarchs, the nature of the prophets, and the justice of God. I don't remember our driver's name, so I'm going to call him Omar. We were in bustling capitol traffic, winding our way among many important government buildings, when Omar brought up the subject of Islamic terrorism.

"If I were to murder many people," he said, "even if I claimed I was on jihad, there is no way God could forgive me for that."

"No way to get forgiveness at all?" I asked.

"No," he said, "because if I murder someone, there can be no restitution. If I steal from you, you can get restitution. I can pay you back what was taken. I can be punished in a way that would give you satisfaction. But if I kill you . . ."

I smiled to mask my nerves.

"That is not something I can make restitution for. So if you cannot forgive me, then God cannot forgive me."

"So when a terrorist gets to heaven, what happens? He doesn't get paradise?"

22

"No," Omar said. "There is no way God can let him enter. Murder is so horrible that God cannot forgive it."

On the one hand, I really appreciated how strong a view of justice Omar appeared to have. He rightly knew that murder was a serious offense. In the Bible God forbids it, of course, but he does seem to provide some measures of restitution, mainly in the form of capital punishment. And yet, I could grant his point that "forgiveness" may be a different sort of animal altogether than simply "restitution."

"In Christianity," I said, "we believe that God can forgive anything, so long as someone believes in Jesus Christ."

Omar replied, not angrily or argumentatively, but straightforwardly, "God cannot forgive these things because they are too terrible."

"What do you believe about Jesus, though?" Jonathan asked. "That he was a prophet?"

"Yes," replied Omar, nodding. He had a great way of gesturing with his right hand while talking, almost as if directing an invisible orchestra, while his left hand gripped the steering wheel. "Jesus is one of God's prophets. Like Moses and Abraham and Jacob."

"You don't believe he died for people's sins?"

"On the cross? No."

"What happened to him?" I said.

"God took him into heaven."

At some point, and I don't know how we got there, because it was a very short ride to our destination, we began talking about some of those prophets and comparing the Old Testament narratives with what he had been taught about them. Most of the basic storylines were the same.

For instance, he did believe that Abraham took his son Isaac up a mountain to sacrifice him at God's command, but that in the end, God provided a ram in the thicket as the substitutionary sacrifice. The appearance of that ram basically rescued Isaac.

For Muslims like Omar, this is a wonderful example of the kindness of God. For Christians, it is certainly that but it is also a foreshadow of the mission of Jesus Christ, who was sacrificed in our place, satisfying the justice of God and sparing our lives.

"Doesn't that story make you think of what Christians believe about Jesus?" I asked.

"I can see what you're saying," Omar said. "It is interesting."

We didn't press our friend for any kind of response or ask him to pray any kind of prayer. But before we exited the cab, we made sure that he had heard that God can and does forgive sins—even the worst kinds of sins—because he has punished them at the cross where his Son Jesus died, paying the penalty for these sins.

I've thought about that encounter a lot over the last couple of years, praying for Omar that the seed planted for this good news took root and that perhaps he was compelled to look further into information about Jesus. But I also think about what that encounter taught me about human nature and religious ideology and people's various views of God.

See, it is much easier today to dismiss what others believe in, because we live in the culture of sound bites and caricatures. Very few people are actually studying what their opponents believe about religious subjects, or even about political or cultural issues, because this is the age of snark, of clickbait, of slogans. I don't have to interact with what you believe to reject it; I don't even have to *know* what you actually believe. All I have to do, really, is turn your beliefs into a superficial catchphrase. In the field of logic, they call this "creating a strawman."

So for instance, you've probably heard phrases—or even said them—such as "I don't believe in magical sky fairies," or "I don't believe in old men in outer space who grant wishes."

Well, guess what? Christians don't believe in sky fairies or elderly wish-granting spacemen either.

Everyone Agrees on the "Idea" of God

In fact, one of the best ways to engage in substantive religious conversations with people who claim not to believe in God is simply to ask them to describe the deity they don't believe in. More than likely, you will be able to tell them you don't believe in that guy either.

What I learned from Omar the cab driver is that Islamic theology is more nuanced than the version criticized by Christians on Facebook or analyzed by Fox News. And I also learned that Omar, like most people, has a strong sense of justice built into his belief system.

Omar could not fathom the idea of a God who could forgive murder. I don't think this is unique at all. In fact, I think we find this "justice of God" concept at work both in the liberal theology of progressive Christianity and in the general relativism and subjectivism found among many atheists. Nearly every sane person either believes in a God who takes evil seriously or believes that *if* God exists, he ought to.

In the progressive wing of Christian faith, the mercy and kindness of God is highlighted, often to the distortion or marginalization of the holiness of God as depicted in Scripture, so the common perception is that the progressives' God is quite tolerant. But at the same time, progressives are very interested in justice, in overcoming evil, and in driving out spiritual darkness. They, like all biblical Christians, believe in a just God. They may not believe in hell or in wrath, and they may not talk too much about sin, but they do believe there are things that are wrong and that God takes these wrong things seriously.

Similarly, even logically consistent atheists understand the concept of a God who takes evil seriously. Evil is a serious problem for atheism, which is why today's "new atheists" expend lots of rhetorical and philosophical energy on exposing the evils of Christendom and religion in general. They do not believe in any divine being, of course, but they will acknowledge that if there *were* a God, he would have a lot of explaining to do. And if there were a God who sent evil people to a place like hell, nearly every atheist would admit that people like Adolf Hitler and Jeffrey Dahmer would deserve to go there.

It turns out that the idea of God's holiness is not as foreign a concept as many people think. All of us are hardwired for justice, for moral absolutism. You can prove this by stealing an atheist's grandma's VCR. (Because their grandma likely still has a VCR.) They probably will not think this is an okay thing to do. Or, if you really want to see someone's sense of right and wrong revealed, simply share your view concerning gay marriage. This cultural hot button has become the issue of our day to determine who's "right" and who's "wrong."

Of course, adherents of the major world religions will disagree with many irreligious people on what is actually right and wrong, but we agree with all sane persons in the world that there *is* such a thing as right and wrong. Atheists may attribute morality to our evolved cultural consciousness (or whatever), but whatever has been designated as the basis for their moral standard is their functional god. We religionists, however, believe that in fact there is a very real God who has been quite specific on what is right and what is wrong and that he will not leave those who fail to order their lives accordingly unpunished. Factoring in a few distinctions unique to each religion, all three of the major monotheistic religions—Judaism, Christianity, and Islam—believe that God takes sin seriously and will sooner or later do something about it.

Does this mean, then, that Jews, Christians, and Muslims worship the same God? While all three agree that God is holy, each makes unique truth claims that distinguish their view of the one God from the others.

Goodness, Gracious

I really appreciated that Omar took sin so seriously. I also liked that he believed God could be forgiving. Both of these truths—that God is holy and that God forgives—are important to understanding the one true God, and yet the three monotheistic religions each approach holiness and forgiveness differently.

In Omar's religious worldview, God could not under any circumstances forgive sins of great gravity like murder. I'm going to assume Omar would also include things like rape and sexual abuse in this category. He is on the right track.

But as a Christian, I don't like that he could not conceive of any other alternative to this view of God. God forgives some sins but not others? Christians believe that God forgives some people but not others. This is obviously not the same thing. Christians believe that some people who commit murder will go to heaven, and they believe that some people who do not commit murder will not. So what makes the difference?

The first thing to say is that, from the Christian perspective, it is not the type of sin that one commits that deserves punishment from a holy God but the presence of sin itself. Because God is perfectly holy, we believe, the sin of gossip deserves wrath just as the sin of murder does. Now, we do acknowledge that murder is a more serious sin than gossip. We can see the degrees of types of sins in the real-world punishments God commands for corresponding offenses in the Old Testament books of Leviticus and Deuteronomy. But this does not mean that there are some sins God "lets slide" while there are others he cannot under any circumstances forgive.

The apostle Paul makes this point in his letter to the Romans:

As it is written: "None is righteous, no, not one; no one understands; no one seeks for God. All have turned aside; together they have become worthless; no one does good, not even one". . . for all have sinned and fall short of the glory of God. (Rom. 3:10–12, 23)

This assertion indicts everyone, the gossip and the murderer, the thief and the abuser, the gluttonous and the gay. It indicts both religious people and irreligious people. And, yes, it includes those who mark "Christian" on religious surveys as well as those who mark "Jewish" or "Muslim." Compared to the light of God's holiness, every human being stands guilty, and God "will by no means clear the guilty" (Nah. 1:3).

So the Christian view holds the same seriousness about sin as Islam, only more so, because it leaves no wiggle room in terms of degrees of sin.

But this is not all there is to believe about the Christian God.

We see God's justice and judgment, the perfect application of his holy wrath, throughout the Bible, in both Old and New Testaments. But we also see the perfect application of his holy love. Consider the following:

- "The LORD is slow to anger" (Nah. 1:3, the same passage where we learn he will not clear the guilty).
- "Give thanks to the LORD, for he is good, for his steadfast love endures forever" (Ps. 136:1).
- "Great is your mercy, O LORD" (Ps. 119:156).
- "Who is a God like you, pardoning iniquity and passing over transgression?" (Mic. 7:18).

- "For the grace of God has appeared, bringing salvation for all people" (Titus 2:11).
- "God [is] rich in mercy" (Eph. 2:4).
- "God is love" (1 John 4:8).

The God that Christians believe in is perfectly holy and gracious. Of course, both Muslims and Jews believe that God can forgive sins. That part is not unique to Christianity. But *how* he forgives sin is something entirely different.

See, in every other religion, including in the other two major monotheistic religions, the way one receives pardon from God is through some kind of achievement—doing enough good works, faithfully attending worship services, "having your heart in the right place," or even simply being or becoming a member of the religion. Only Christianity says that while all those things are good things, they cannot earn us the forgiveness of sins.

Again, this is not because good works or church attendance or identifying with the Christian religion are bad things. It is only because all of our religious and spiritual efforts will always be tainted somewhat by our guilty hearts. We have self-interested motives and imperfect practices. This is a perfectly holy God we have here!

Thus, in every other religion where God is said to forgive, he has to do so by in some way compromising his holiness. In other words, he sort of tips the scales toward his mercy and away from his righteousness. He kind of "bends the rules." He sacrifices one part of himself in order that we might take advantage of another.

But the God that Christians worship does not compromise one bit. He bends no rules. In fact, he punishes every single sin. Not a single sin throughout all of history slips through the cracks.

So how can he forgive sinners like us while maintaining the perfection of his holiness?

He puts our sin on Jesus Christ.

God has declared that he will by no means clear the guilty. So he instead makes guilty people righteous. But to do this in a way that is just, he must make a righteous person guilty. And he accomplishes this, the Bible reveals, by punishing our sin by punishing his Son Jesus.

Jesus then goes to the cross as personally sinless but nevertheless bearing the sins of the world, willingly and undeservedly taking upon himself the condemnation that we all deserve but wish to avoid.

In this way, all sin is accounted for. Whether by the wrath of hell or by the wrath of the cross, every single sin is accounted for.

And in this way, the grace of God is revealed. Christians therefore believe that if anyone wants to stand before a holy God and be declared holy enough to escape judgment, they must reject trust in their own good works and instead accept the good work of Jesus Christ as their own.

The cross of Jesus Christ, then, shows us how God is both perfectly holy and perfectly loving, totally just and yet totally gracious. It is through the cross of Christ that God, according to the apostle Paul, "[showed] his righteousness at the present time, so that he might be just and the justifier of the one who has faith in Jesus" (Rom.

3:26). Former Muslim—now a Christian pastor—Thabiti Anyabwile puts it this way:

> By Jesus' sacrifice, God reveals and defends His justice in two ways. First, Jesus' suffering for the sins of His people means that any sins unpunished beforehand are now fully punished in Christ. God leaves no sin unpunished. Mercy and grace do not come at the expense of justice. Second, because the sins of the faithful are fully punished in Jesus, God may justly declare righteous those who have faith in Jesus. That's what it means to be justified in God's sight—to be declared righteous by faith in Jesus. The cross, rightly understood, is God's own answer to any objection that He is unfair to substitute Jesus for the unrighteous.[1]

The God of Islam and Judaism is just. But only through a variety of human religious effort could he be said to be a justifier. The Christian God is both *just* and *justifier*, and he does his justifying as an act of sheer grace, forgiving sinners not by their obedience (because we could never obey well enough) but by Christ's.

This may seem like a rather thin line to draw, especially between Christianity's view of God and Judaism's view, but through the lens of the subsequent revelation of the New Testament we can see that what the God of Judaism and Islam demands, the God of Christianity both demands and *provides*. We will explore more deeply how God does this in chapter 7, but we will keep coming back chapter after chapter to the concept of grace, because, with all due

1. Thabiti Anyabwile, *The Gospel for Muslims* (Chicago: Moody, 2010), 75–76.

respect to other religions' claims of salvation, only Christianity offers salvation by grace.

You can find a loving conception of monotheism in both Judaism and Islam, but only in Christianity does this love manifest itself in a one-way work of salvation of sinners apart from religious effort. For this reason, C. S. Lewis has famously said of Christian faith, "We trust not because 'a God' exists, but because *this* God exists."[2]

There are, of course, many Jews, Muslims, and Christians who believe all three faiths worship the same God, just through different expressions. We see this view suggested even in the Muslim's Koran:

> Do not dispute other than in a good way with the people of Scripture, except for those of them who do evil; and say: "We have faith in that which has been revealed to us and revealed to you. Our God and your God are One, and to Him we submit [ourselves]." (Surah 29:46)

Jews and Christians, also, have much good theology in common. It has become common among people in both faiths to refer to "Judeo-Christian values." This is a real thing, and in many cases, a completely legitimate expression. In a 2007 interview, President George W. Bush said, "I believe in an almighty God, and I believe that all the world, whether they be Muslim, Christian, or any other religion, prays to the same God. That's what I believe."[3]

2. C. S. Lewis, "On Obstinacy in Belief," in *"The World's Last Night" and Other Essays* (San Diego: Harcourt, 1988), 25.

3. Mona Moussly, "Bush Denies He Is an 'Enemy of Islam,'" *Al Arabiya News* (October 5, 2007), http://www.alarabiya.net/articles/2007/10/05/39989.html.

This belief is practically mainstream within all three of these faith traditions.

But I think we come at this answer too easily, too thoughtlessly, simply assuming that because these three religions—Judaism, Christianity, and Islam—are all monotheistic and share some historical heritage, they must worship the same God. In truth, lots of people worshiping one God does not mean they are worshiping the same God.

Do Jews and Christians Worship the Same God?

This is a very complex question, actually, but the short answer is no.

You may flinch at such an assertion. It is not a necessarily popular belief, even within evangelical Christianity, where many simply believe Jews worship what they know of God. It is said that they worship the one true God but simply have an incomplete vision of him. But couldn't this be said of any religious faith whose object of worship bears striking similarities to the God whom Christians worship?

Complicating the question are the various threads within both Judaism and Christianity. One Jewish scholar has said, "The fact is that there is no single Jewish understanding of God."[4] This makes it difficult to distinguish Christianity from Judaism, if only because we aren't dealing with Judaism so much as Judaisms. On the other hand, Christianity has remained almost entirely unified for two thousand years

4. Alon Goshen-Gottstein, "God Between Christians and Jews—Is it the Same God?" Paper presented at the Yale Center for Faith and Culture, http://faith.yale.edu/sites/default/files/goshen_final_paper_0.pdf.

on the central matters of its theological claims. But one stark contrast between the Christian view of God and the Jewish view is this thing called grace.

Now, drawing the line at the concept of grace may seem too narrow a division. The God revealed in the Jewish Tanakh displays abundant grace constantly. Christians would affirm that. We do not believe that the God of the Old Testament is different from the God of the New Testament. We affirm with our Jewish forebears that there is one God. And we affirm that grace is abundant throughout the Tanakh. We simply believe that the New Testament provides the fuller revelation necessary to understand the Old. The unity between the two books demonstrates not just that God has always been gracious but that God has also always been gracious through his eternal plan for salvation in Jesus Christ.

Christians believe that we must believe about God what God has revealed about himself, and that to disbelieve what God has revealed about himself and to worship some more preferred version of God is in fact to worship an idol. In the historic account of the children of Israel worshiping the golden calf, in fact, we see that Aaron and the Israelites attributed their worship of this false god to God (Exod. 32:5).

When Christians talk about grace, however, the thing that makes Christianity utterly unique among all faiths, we aren't simply referring to a disposition of God or a personality trait. We are referring to those things too, of course, but more specifically we are referring to the way God has expressed his grace, namely through the person and work of Jesus Christ.

It is at Jesus, in fact, that Judaism and Christianity part theological ways.

This is not simply a matter of opinion. It is a matter of diametrically opposed truth claims. And we see this opposition recurring over and over again throughout the teaching ministry of Jesus depicted in the Gospels of the New Testament.

In John 8, orthodox Jewish leaders are once again spying on Jesus, trying to trip him up, expose him, defame him, and shame him. You have to understand that the Pharisees of Jesus's day were not fringe characters in the Jewish religion. They were the religious elite, but theologically speaking they represented mainstream, "contemporary" Judaism. They shared much of the same theology as Jesus and his disciples. The Pharisees represented the faithful reading of the Hebrew Scriptures. They believed in the covenantal history, in a future resurrection, and in applying the revelation of God to everyday life. They would be the equivalent, probably, of the fundamentalist strain of Christianity today—culturally zealous and a little rough around the edges, but on all the majors, pretty much theologically correct.

So it is no little thing that Jesus and the Pharisees butt heads here in John 8. This is not simply a clash between nice Jesus and mean leaders. It is much more than that. It is a fundamental disagreement on the very identity of God.

Jesus is doing what Jesus always does: making everything about himself. In this instance, he claims to be the Judge, the Light of the World, the Way to freedom from sin, and a few other equally provocative things. This is not the kind of thing a normal religious leader says. We don't tend to take seriously religious leaders who make such claims about themselves.

Jesus then says something even stranger:

> "Your father Abraham rejoiced that he would see my day. He saw it and was glad." So the Jews said to him, "You are not yet fifty years old, and have you seen Abraham?" Jesus said to them, "Truly, truly, I say to you, before Abraham was, I am." (John 8:56–58)

What does he mean?

Jesus is saying two incredible things here. First, he claims to have been in existence before Abraham. This is an overt claim to preexistence, in fact to eternality and omnipresence. And by saying "I am"—asserting that thousands of years ago, not only *was* he, but he *currently is*—he is applying the sacred name of Yahweh ("I AM") to himself. This may sound subtle to modern readers but it's not subtle at all. Jesus is in fact claiming to be God. We know the orthodox Jews understood him to be making this claim, because the very next thing they do (v. 59) is pick up stones to kill him, which is exactly what any good first-century Jew would feel inclined to do when confronted with such blatant blasphemy.

Again, this is not merely a matter of opinion. This is not simply a case of the Jewish theologians worshiping the same God in a different way. If Jesus is in fact God, and you try to kill him, how could you say in any legitimate way that you worship and believe in God?

Jesus makes this very point, actually, earlier in the same chapter.

Jesus said to them, "If you were Abraham's children, you would be doing the works Abraham did, but now you seek to kill me, a man who has told you the truth that I heard from God. This is not what Abraham did. You are doing the works your father did." They said to him, "We were not born of sexual immorality. We have one Father—even God." Jesus said to them, "If God were your Father, you would love me, for I came from God and I am here. I came not of my own accord, but he sent me. Why do you not understand what I say? It is because you cannot bear to hear my word. You are of your father the devil, and your will is to do your father's desires. He was a murderer from the beginning, and does not stand in the truth, because there is no truth in him. When he lies, he speaks out of his own character, for he is a liar and the father of lies. But because I tell the truth, you do not believe me. Which one of you convicts me of sin? If I tell the truth, why do you not believe me? Whoever is of God hears the words of God. The reason why you do not hear them is that you are not of God." (vv. 39–47)

To summarize, Jesus is saying that if somebody worshiped the true God they would worship *him*, because he is of the same nature as the true God. And he is saying that if anyone rejects him they reject the one true God. And further, he is saying that if anyone—including these orthodox Jews—does not believe in him they are more aligned with the enemy of God, Satan himself.

I share that lengthy passage so you will see that I am not making this up. Jesus said it. And you are welcome to disagree, and you are welcome to be offended. But you should plainly see that Jesus is himself saying that to reject him is to reject God, deny the truth, and reveal oneself as being "not of God."

In John 10:30, Jesus doubles down on these claims, and says, "I and the Father are one." Once again, the Jewish theologians take up stones to murder him, which they would not have done if all he meant was that he and God were "on the same team." Verse 33 makes their motive explicit: "The Jews answered him, 'It is not for a good work that we are going to stone you but for blasphemy, because you, being a man, make yourself God.'"

I believe it is very important that we understand this important contrast if we want to understand both orthodox Christianity and the orthodox Judaism that developed from the time of Christ onward. The conflict between Jesus and the unbelieving Jews of his day did not rise or fall on how nice Jesus was compared to how mean the Pharisees were. That's a very superficial reading of Jesus's relationship with the religious leaders, which is probably why it's the most common understanding in the secular world of why Jesus was killed.

But while Jesus was a faithful and religious Jew, his beef with the Pharisees and scribes is not simply some intramural personality clash. It is a fundamental clash of worldviews. Namely, Jesus is orienting the world around himself, putting himself in the center of everything. He is in fact claiming to be God. And if he is right—as I believe he is—then to disagree with him is to disagree with God. To deny him is to deny God. To reject him is to reject God. And to worship God at the exclusion of Jesus is to worship another god altogether.

Christians believe that God became flesh in the person of Jesus Christ, who was conceived by the Holy Spirit in the womb of a virgin named Mary, and who grew and developed into mature, real, tangible manhood.

So, do Jews worship the same God as Christians? The Christian faith has its roots in the Jewish culture and religion, and the two faith traditions share a common sacred history, but as it really counts—meaning, as it really applies to a relationship with the supreme deity who actually exists—the answer is no. Because if God has revealed himself in Jesus Christ, if indeed Jesus Christ is God, if indeed God is a Trinity, then to reject these truths about his very nature—which is not the same as being mistaken about certain attributes of God or not understanding certain aspects of his personality—means rejecting God himself.

Jesus Christ makes all the difference in the world.

Putting Skin in the Game

It is true that one general commonality between Judaism, Christianity, and Islam is the personal nature of the relationship that is said to be possible between God and humanity. In each of these religions, God is seen as "coming near" to people. How he does this differs, but there is a striking shared sense of a "personal God."

In that same 2007 interview with Al Arabiya news, President Bush also said this:

> I believe there is a universal God. I believe the God that the Muslim prays to is the same God that I pray to.

After all, we all came from Abraham. I believe in that universality.[5]

It is interesting that the president mentions Abraham. It is often said that the major monotheistic religions are complementary "Abrahamic traditions." They share that universality Bush refers to. It's with the historic account of Abraham, in fact, that we see one of the most important traits of the one true God: his relationality.

Islam of course generally affirms the Abrahamic history of the Hebrew scriptures, but it is Judaism and Christianity that follow the narrative most closely.

When Abram—later renamed "Abraham" by God himself—enters the biblical scene, civilization has once again degenerated after the great flood of Noah's day. The most emblematic historical moment in this postdiluvian world is the construction of the Tower of Babel, which the Bible tells us is an extreme exercise in monumental hubris. When God disperses the people of that time into numerous tongues—and thus, tribes—civilization continues to spread but so does animosity, barbarism, and paganism. The world is full of polytheistic idolatry, and this fellow Abram is right in the thick of it, minding his own business, when God shows up.

> Now the LORD said to Abram, "Go from your country and your kindred and your father's house to the land that I will show you. And I will make of you a great nation, and I will bless you and make your name great, so that you will be a blessing. I will bless those who bless you, and him who

5. Moussly, "Bush Denies He Is an 'Enemy of Islam.'"

dishonors you I will curse, and in you all the families of the earth shall be blessed." (Gen. 12:1–3)

The promise we find in this passage is the beginning of God's covenant with Abraham, a commitment to a relationship that is personal and eternal. This covenant is unlike any relationship any person ever before was said to have with any of the so-called gods the world's cultures worshiped. This God was initiating a relationship with this person, and the relationship was of the nature that Abraham and God could be called *friends*!

> Did you not, our God, drive out the inhabitants of this land before your people Israel, and give it forever to the descendants of Abraham your friend? (2 Chron. 20:7)

>> But you, Israel, my servant,
>> Jacob, whom I have chosen,
>> the offspring of Abraham, my friend. (Isa. 41:8)

> "Abraham believed God, and it was counted to him as righteousness"—and he was called a friend of God. (James 2:23)

To understand the significance of this, you really do have to see how people worshiped in this age. Abram lived not just in an idolatrous culture but in a desperately wicked one. He resided in Ur of the Chaldeans with his brothers in his father Terah's home. Ur is a pagan place. And all of the names of the people here in Abram's family, including his wife, Sarai, indicate they come from a tribal people who worship the moon. And what archaeologists and historians have been able to uncover about these people in Ur, of which Abram was almost certainly a part, was that they carried out horrific atrocities in their moon worship, including sexual depravity and human sacrifice. It's likely Abram witnessed such things; they were a normal part of his culture.

So Abraham was a polytheistic, spiritually wicked pagan man. He wasn't sitting on his rooftop every day reading his *Jesus Calling* devotional book, drinking coffee from his "YHWH Is My Homeboy" mug. He didn't know God, he didn't want God, and he didn't seek God. But God knew him, wanted him, and sought him.

God saw this pagan, idolatrous, moon-worshiping dude Abram and said, "This guy is totally hopeless, totally clueless, totally spirit-less. Now *that* I can work with," and he redeemed him. This is that one-directional, gracious initiative that distinguishes the God of the Bible from all other alleged deities. We know, in fact, that Abraham was not saved by God because he was a good person, because he was not a good person when God called him. And we also know this because the Bible says it. Genesis 15:6 tells us that Abraham's salvation was not based on his works but rather God's grace received through faith. The New Testament later affirms this (Rom. 4:3).

Judaism obviously has Genesis 15:6 and the entire Abrahamic narrative in their Bible. But they do not have the whole story. Once again, we see that Jesus Christ is the dividing line, not just between religious perspectives but between opposing truth claims.

In every other religion people seek God. Only in Christianity does God seek people. Judaism's God certainly initiates with humans, but there is still that distance. When the prophetic door closes at the end of the biblical book of Malachi, Judaism's God stops speaking; the revelation is done. But when the pages of the New Testament begin, the one true God of Israel continues to speak.

But it's even more exciting than that. He actually comes down and lets you look him in the eye. It is actually this kind of face-to-face personal relationship that the Old Testament pages are pointing to, hinting at, and foreshadowing.

Abraham's faith, not his obedience, is credited to him as righteousness. In the New Testament book that most explicitly fleshes out the meaning of the Jewish Bible, Abraham is commended for this humble faith. It is his trust in God that receives for him the holiness he needs to please God. In that book, we read, "Now faith is the assurance of things hoped for, the conviction of things not seen" (Heb. 11:1).

So what was the vision Abram saw that he believed in? What would cause him to leave all that he knew, all that he held dear, all that seemed certain in his life to follow God into the place he had yet to be shown (Gen. 12:1)? Through his faith, he was seeing something he could not see.

Jesus says this vision was of him: "Your father Abraham rejoiced that he would see my day. He saw it and was glad" (John 8:56).

Once again, Jesus makes all the difference.

See, in Christianity, what we have is not simply a personal God who seeks relationship with humankind but the personal God who seeks relationship by *becoming a man*. This is completely incompatible with the truth claims of the

Judaism of Jesus's day and of today, which sees much that it admires and even affirms in Christian heritage and morality but sees the radical claims of Jesus Christ as something to be utterly rejected. The Jewish religion denies that Jesus Christ is both Lord and Savior. And as Jesus himself says, to disbelieve in him is to disbelieve in God.

The Christian doctrine of incarnation draws a very visible line in the religious sand. If one does not affirm that Jesus is God, one does not worship the same God as Christians.

But the monotheistic distinctions are even more specific than that, because Christianity's understanding of God's nature is fundamentally and radically different from Judaism's and Islam's. Jacob Neusner says, "In its classical sources, normative Judaism does not recognize any other religion as monotheistic like itself."[6] This is largely the case because Christianity worships three Persons as one God.

And in fact, Christianity's Trinitarianism answers an elemental ache in the human soul. Deep down, we long for justice and for forgiveness, and God provides through his Triune self.

I wish I'd said that to Omar the cab driver. I wish I'd told him that the heavenly Father can forgive these terrible sins against us because his Son had taken the terrible justice—indeed, paid the ultimate price of death—to make the restitution he didn't think was possible. And I would've told him that the Holy Spirit then applies this payment to

6. Jacob Neusner, "Do Monotheist Religions Worship the Same God? A Perspective on Classical Judaism," *Do Jews, Christians, and Muslims Worship the Same God?* (Nashville: Abingdon, 2012), 28.

anyone who will trust in the Son. It's like getting saved by a ram in the thicket.

And I also wished I'd told him that the Trinity, in fact, speaks in a much greater way to the human need to "be square" with both God and each other.

+   +   +   +   **2**   +

When 1 + 1 + 1 = 1

HOW THE REALITY OF THE TRINITY ANSWERS DEEP HUMAN LONGING

When I was a sophomore in high school, I sat in the cafeteria at lunchtime with a few other guys who were just like me and not like me at all.

I'll try to explain.

Our school lunchroom probably looked a lot like many other suburban lunchrooms across the country, each table representing a given segment of the high school population. At one table sat the jocks, at another the skaters, at another the nerds, still another the band geeks, and so on and so forth. In our suburban Houston cafeteria there was a fairly visible segmentation across racial lines as well. Black kids tended to sit all together, as did Asian kids and Hispanic kids. But our table was a little different. Nearly every day I sat and ate bad burritos or soggy pizza alongside my best friend Eric (who was Hispanic), as well as Babar (Middle Eastern), Tam (Vietnamese), Charles (African American), and Maruf (Indian).

I would like to say that we sat together as part of some conscious effort at racial unity. In reality, we each sort of represented a sense of alienation from our respective tribes. What we had in common was the fact that we had little in common with the majority population. None of us were exactly jocks (although we also shared PE together and made a pretty effective basketball team, believe it or not), but we weren't quite nerds either. We weren't popular kids but we weren't pathetic bully-bait either. We just kind of *were*. But we had a great time talking about religion (only two of us were Christians), movies, sports, and in general just cutting up and laughing.

On the surface, we had very little in common. Underneath, we were kindred spirits. And as I look back on that ordinary little lunch table, I think of how we brought out different things in each other. Some of us were closer friends than others, but we "played well together." There was something we each—pardon the pun—*brought to the table* that made the table more than the sum of its parts. Charles had a way of drily responding to my ribbing that made Eric laugh harder than anything else. Babar had a way of dramatically reacting to everything that made us enjoy egging him on. And when we discussed deeper things—faith, especially—the various perspectives and religions represented at the table made for a better sharpening of all of our viewpoints.

The collaborative personality of our table makes me think of C. S. Lewis's thoughts about friendship:

> In each of my friends there is something that only some other friend can fully bring out. By myself I am not large enough to call the whole man into activity; I want other lights than my own to show all his facets.[1]

In that same discussion, Lewis talks about how after their mutual friend Charles Williams died, he did not really get more of his friend J. R. R. Tolkien but actually less, because Williams had brought out so much more of Tolkien. Each member of their friend circle (the Inklings) brought out things in each of the others that made the circle more full, more lively, more their truest individual selves.

The Trinity that Christians know is a lot like that.

No, we don't believe that any individual Person of the Trinity is somehow deficient in and of themselves. Certainly none of them can die. But there is something about their three-in-oneness that enhances—or, to use the biblical word, *glorifies*—the beauty and Personhood of each individual Person. The Father relates to the Son and the Spirit, the Son relates to the Father and the Spirit, and the Spirit relates to the Father and the Son in diverse but mutually exalting ways that make each fully

1. C. S. Lewis, *The Four Loves* (Orlando, FL: Harcourt Brace, 1991), 61.

sufficient individual Person of the Godhead somehow more glorious.

But I'm getting ahead of myself.

Three Wholes Adding Up to One

"I could never worship a God who sends people to hell."

I'm sure you've heard this sentiment before, or others very similar to it. It would seem that many people who reject the idea of the Christian God do so not because they have found the Christian God irrational but rather unnecessary, or even *distasteful*. The complementary line of thinking goes something like this: *I could believe in God, but only if he held to my own ideas and values.*

Many people seem completely clear on the kind of God they could worship and couldn't—that is, until you start giving a fuller sense of the parts of God they are rejecting. Then the objection isn't quite so automatic.

For instance, when somebody objects to the idea that God would punish someone in an eternal place of torment like hell, they are typically thinking of all the nice people they know who aren't believers. With such good people in mind, the idea of a judgmental God seems so . . . well, *judgmental*. But, as we discussed earlier, bring up Adolf Hitler or Jeffrey Dahmer or Adam Lanza, and the idea suddenly seems somewhat less objectionable. Suddenly they can admit there is a logic to the idea of eternal punishment for very bad people.

What's happened? They had previously shrunk their view of God to their personal way of thinking, which is very specific, very individual, and therefore very narrow. The God most people want, even in their claims of tolerance and open-mindedness, turns out to be very narrow-minded indeed. He is simply a projection of themselves. But when more data is added to the line of thinking—when the view can be expanded a bit—we find many people adjusting, finding ways to revise their views. The true God is always keeping us on our heels.

Thinking about God is almost always like this. It has been said that in the beginning, God made man in his own image, and man has been trying to return the favor ever since!

The kind of God we want to worship is the kind who is pretty much exactly like us—the kind of God who shares our thinking, our preferences, and our tastes. And then we encounter the real God—from the words in the Bible and the Christian teaching that comes from it—and our mind is expanded. We must either find new reasons to reject him or we must surrender our objections altogether.

I think the Christian teaching on the idea called the Trinity is like this. We do not have the mental capacity to "run the numbers" on this idea. It does not seem to add up. One plus one plus one equals . . . one? How does that make any sense? "I cannot believe in a God who expects us to believe he is three in one," says the critic.

The Trinitarian God offends our sense of reason and logic. He seems utterly impractical. How much more appealing Christianity might seem if it stopped insisting on this bizarre spiritual arithmetic of *three wholes adding up to one!*

And beyond that, even if you could somehow get over the irrationality of it all, there is still the matter of the Trinity's utter impracticality. What difference in the world could the Trinity make? There doesn't seem to be any reason at all *in* it, and there doesn't seem to be much reason at all *for* it.

Ah, but this kind of thinking lacks the fuller picture! The truth is, once we get at the greater perspective, the Christian view of a Triune God is not only logical it is incredibly necessary. The doctrine of the Trinity, in fact, explains the deepest longings of the human heart.

When we "nutshell" the ways Christianity is different from every other religion, we see very quickly that the Christian faith stands out in its understanding of the very nature of God. Like the other major monotheistic religions, Christians believe there is only one God. All other gods are false gods—inanimate idols at best, demonic forces at worst.

And yet Christianity's monotheism remains provocative, because the Christian believes the Bible teaches that this one God eternally exists in three divine Persons. This is not so in Judaism, which derives its understanding of God from the same texts the Christians call the Old Testament. And it is not so in Islam, which agrees that there is one true God but denies that God may have any offspring (whether "eternally begotten," as Christians believe the Son of God to be, or human).

In the teachings of Mormonism and the Jehovah's Witnesses, there is more accommodation made between God being one and Jesus being divine, but the way these religions "do the math" results in an underlying polytheism.

For instance, Mormons believe that Jesus is just one of many "sons of God," that he actually ascended to godhood through his obedience to the Father, and that we may ascend to godhood ourselves by our own faithfulness. In Jehovah's Witness teaching, Jesus is understood to be not the eternally begotten Son of God, "very God of very God" as the historic Christian creeds say, but simply one of multiple divine beings. They famously mistranslate John 1:1 to read, "In the beginning the Word was, and the Word was with God, and the Word was *a god*."[2] (An accurate translation of that verse tells us that the Word that was with God "*was* God.")

These are the two primary categories with which non-Christian religions that draw their teaching (at least in part) from the Bible work. They either hold to God's "oneness" while rejecting his "three-ness" or they seek to accommodate his three-ness by fudging on the oneness. To put it charitably, they have found the doctrine of the Trinity lacking in logic and have opted for either a non-Trinitarian monotheism or a quasi-Trinitarian polytheism. In this sense, they simply align with the great mass of religious ideology remaining. Christianity's understanding of God stands alone.

Only Christianity teaches the Trinity. Only Christianity teaches that there is, yes, only one God, and that this one God exists in three Persons. There are not three gods, but one. And there is not one God who alternately manifests as

2. The New World Translation (Watchtower). Emphasis added. For more background on this misinterpretation of essential biblical teaching, see http://carm.org/religious-movements/jehovahs-witnesses/john-11-word-was-god.

three Persons. The three Persons who are God—Father, Son, and Holy Spirit—are each individually fully, equally, eternally God. They are each of the same substance, or essence, as the other, and yet they are distinctively three. Nevertheless, they are together one God. Now, when Christians say that God exists eternally as a Trinity of *divine persons* they do not mean "creatures," much less "human beings." By *person* we may mean "individuals" or "figures." But theologians have come to settle on that word "person" in order to convey the reality that each Person of the Triune God has a distinct personality, despite sharing with the others the same essence and despite the three together being one God.

The Biblical Reality of the Trinity

All of that's well and good, you may be thinking right now, *but you promised to explain the* why *of the Trinity, not just the* what. Well, you're right. Though I can't promise that you will find my explanations agreeable, I do hope they'll give you a greater sense of why the Christian view of the Trinity is both necessary and compelling.

First of all, Christians find the doctrine of the Trinity necessary because they see this doctrine in the Bible. In Deuteronomy 6:4, we find the traditional Hebrew declaration called the Shema, in which God's faithful children affirm that "The LORD our God, the LORD is one." There is and has always been only one God. Faithful Christians, like faithful Jews, affirm this important truth. But perhaps as early as Genesis 1:26, we see some evidence of multiplicity in this oneness. In that verse, God speaks to himself and refers to himself in the first person plural—"Let *us* make man in *our* image" (emphasis added).

The deity of the One referred to as the Father seems evident throughout the Old and New Testaments. In the pages of the New Testament, however, that same word *Lord* is ascribed to Jesus Christ (as in John 20:28, for instance). John 1:1 tells us that Jesus was there in the beginning, active in creation, saying that he was not only "with God" but "was God." Ditto John 1:18, which says that the only God was at the Father's side. How could one who is also God be with God? The New Testament's Trinitarianism is shining through.

Similarly, Jesus's enemies, no theological lightweights themselves, understood that he was teaching his own equality with God (John 5:18; 10:33). Later on, the apostle Paul states unequivocally that Jesus Christ is "God over all" (Rom. 9:5) and "great God and Savior" (Titus 2:13). He refers to Jesus's equality with God in Philippians 2:6, and says in Colossians 2:9 that the "whole fullness of deity dwells bodily" in him. The apostle who gave us John 1:1 also tells us later that Jesus is the true God (1 John 5:20). The apostle Peter refers to Jesus as God (2 Pet. 1:1). The author of Hebrews does the same (Hebrews 1:3, 8).

We will examine more closely the Christian claim about the divinity of Jesus in chapter 5, but for now we see that Jesus is not taught in the pages of Scripture as simply a human ambassador for God or a specially anointed prophet. His closest followers believed him to be God in the flesh.

Similarly, the Holy Spirit is referred to throughout the Bible as God's divine presence in the world. He is referred to distinctively from the Father and the Son, and yet is also referred to in various places as both "the Spirit of the LORD" and "the Spirit of Christ." The Holy Spirit is sometimes referred to as the "shy" Person of the Trinity, because his role is largely seen as completing the will of the Father in shining the light on Christ, but he carries this out uniquely as a comforter, convicter, and counselor. The Spirit may not occupy as much biblical airtime as the Father and the Son, but he certainly occupies as much airspace! He is fully and coequally God, as well.

In Matthew 28:19, Jesus instructs his followers to baptize in the name (singular) of the Father, Son, and the Holy Spirit, putting the Trinitarian doctrine right inside the teaching of Christ himself. And in 1 Peter 1:1–2, Peter shows us that the Trinitarian God is integral to our understanding of forgiveness, redemption, and salvation. The Father commissions the work of salvation of sinners, the Son accomplishes this work, and the Spirit applies it.

All of that is the general thrust of the entire Bible's teaching on God, which reveals a much more multifaceted monotheism than that of Judaism or Islam. And because Christians take the Bible very seriously, committing to believe whatever is found there, no matter how challenging or counterintuitive, Christians believe in the Trinity. But, of course, only Christians do.

Struggling with the logic problem the Trinity poses, critics of Christianity, especially those who subscribe to other religions, commonly argue that Christians really worship three gods.

No, of course the math doesn't add up. But this is God we're talking about, so we shouldn't necessarily expect our finite minds to ably nail down the logic of the infinite. And here is why the Christian view of the Trinity is both necessary and compelling. It is necessary not just because the Bible teaches it—although that's the primary reason why—but because it gives us a God *completely beyond the bounds of total human understanding*.

Two theologians put it like this:

> When people begin to think about God's triune nature and say, "This doesn't seem logical," in reality it is not a contradiction in logic that they are sensing but something else. They are sensing the strangeness of the doctrine—there is something to this teaching about God that lacks *analogy* to anything else in human experience. It is unfamiliar to think of a being comprised of three Persons. While there may be nothing innately illogical about the idea, it is certainly unheard of in any other sphere of human experience and is thus strange to us. This is what we mean by saying that the so-called *logical* question is not really a logical question but an *analogical* question.[3]

We can know God, sure, but we can't understand God. What I mean is, we can't wrap our minds around God. If God exists, he must be infinitely creative, eternally massive, gloriously big. If there is a God, he must be God! And thus, it is necessary that God be un-figure-out-able. If we

3. Philip Ryken and Michael LeFebvre, *Our Triune God: Living in the Love of the Three-in-One* (Wheaton, IL: Crossway, 2011), 41.

could wrap our puny minds around the nature of God, he wouldn't be God. So the very fact that our logic and rationality fail us when we try to do the math on the triunity of the Godhead gives us a glimpse of just how much Godness there is in God. We should expect our finite rationality to fail when set up like a measuring stick against him.

If you still insist that you couldn't worship a God you can't totally understand, I would suggest that you're really only interested in worshiping yourself. As for me, I couldn't worship a God who so neatly fit into my own little categories. The Trinitarian God blows my mind. So I think Christianity is on to something here.

That's why I think the Trinity is necessary. Because the Bible teaches it, certainly, but also because it is the only concept of God's nature that defies my expectations and understandings.

But to find the necessary Trinity *compelling* requires tracking a bit with another common objection to it. On the more consistently religious side of things, a frequent criticism of the idea of the Trinity is that it just seems so . . . impractical. Sure, as Christians, we believe God exists in three Persons. But what difference does that really make?

The Trinity Explains Our Need for Relationship

It was a dark and (spiritually) stormy night. Jesus was with his closest followers in a garden called Gethsemane, but he may as well have been alone, because they kept falling asleep on him. This was especially distressing because Jesus knew he was only minutes away from his betrayal and arrest, and only hours away from his torture and crucifixion. Luke's Gospel paints a gruesome, unsettling scene, as we see Jesus in such terrible agony he is sweating blood (22:44).

Jesus has spent several years investing in the lives of his friends. He has lived nearly every day right by their side, in the thick of it all, walking and teaching and eating and crying and *being*. Loving them deeply, he has given his life for them, and he's about to literally give up his life for them. Now, in his moment of deep distress, as they snooze and snore, he prays for them alone. But he is not alone.

Earlier Jesus offered another prayer, sometimes called his "high priestly prayer." In it he begins setting the scene for how his special connection with the Father will impact the connection between God and man. He says to his Father:

> But now I am coming to you, and these things I speak in the world, that they may have my joy fulfilled in themselves. I have given them your word, and the world has hated them because they are not of the world, just as I am not of the world. I do not ask that you take them out of the world, but that you keep them from the evil one. They are not of the world, just as I am not of the world. Sanctify them in the truth; your word is truth. As you sent me into the world, so I have sent them into the world. And for their sake I consecrate myself, that they also may be sanctified in truth.
>
> I do not ask for these only, but also for those who will believe in me through their word, that they may all be one, just as you, Father, are in me, and I in you, that they also may be in us, so that the world may believe that you have sent me. The glory that you have given me I have given to them, that they may be one even as we are one, I in them and you in me, that they may become perfectly one, so

that the world may know that you sent me and loved them
even as you loved me. Father, I desire that they also, whom
you have given me, may be with me where I am, to see my
glory that you have given me because you loved me before
the foundation of the world. (John 17:13–24)

I know it's a long passage, but it's important to pay attention at each difficult step of the way, because the entire
universe of human need and the entire cosmos of divine
supply are bound up inside this prayer. What Jesus is tap-
ping into in these words is the very thing we have all been
trying to tap into, really, since we were born.

Jesus begins by praying for his followers' joy—actually,
the joy of himself *transferred into* his followers, fulfilling
their longing for lasting joy. Jesus connects this to the Word
of God given to them—which is joyous in one important
sense because Jesus the Messiah arrived after five hundred
years of prophetic silence and joyous in another because, as
David says in the very first psalm, the authoritative Word
of God is a delight to worshipers. And Jesus himself *is* the
authoritative Word of God.

Jesus prays a beautiful, stunning prayer: "I do not ask
for these only, but also for those who will believe in me
through their word, that they may all be one, just as you,
Father, are in me, and I in you, that they also may be in
us, so that the world may believe that you have sent me
(vv. 20–21).

Jesus isn't just praying for himself and the church, he
is praying for the "future church," for the world of lonely
people longing to hear the good news of relational belong-
ing with God. Jesus speaks to the heart here, addressing our

God-created need for relationship and our sin-created need for reconciliation. Because being restored people means being restored into reflection of the perfect unity of community in the Trinity ("Just as you, Father, are in me, and I in you"), Jesus prays for the Great Commissioning of the church to proclaim the gospel near and far in the hopes of reconciling people to God and thereby creating the reconciling people of the church.

Broken relationships are the worst of the fallout of the Fall. The reason we have such trouble "doing relationships," and the reason the relationships we find ourselves in get complicated by self-interest and conflict is because we are fundamentally and relationally broken. We know we need to be in relationships but we can't seem to get our relationships right. We need the maker of relationships, the originator of relationships, to restore us.

And the Trinity is the reason we crave relational intimacy.

The Trinity Depicts Our Desire for Community

One day, as I was doing some writing in a Panera restaurant, I crashed right into writer's block and started to daydream. Sometimes when I'm stuck with a particular writing piece, I'll just poke around on the internet a little bit and waste time. But when I'm in public I find people-watching unavoidable. That day, as I looked around the restaurant, I noticed lots of people doing people's favorite people-y things. They were eating together, talking, and listening. The place was full, and I scanned table after table full of twos and threes and fours. Some were whispering, some speaking loudly. Some told stories. Others listened intently. One woman laughed quite loudly and slapped her friend playfully on the arm.

At the tables where only one person was seated, the scene was quite boring. No sound, no smile, not much movement. Solitude certainly has its place; it's a necessary discipline for us all. But we were not made to be alone. It says so right in the Bible. I sat alone at my own table, computer screen in my face and a stack of books by my side, but at the tables where two or more were gathered, there was *life*. And it was vibrant and it was diverse. There were people of all shapes and sizes, of different ages and races, from evidently different social classes. Each lively table and the entire restaurant at once—a busy collection of interpersonal relationships and intersecting roles and personalities—gave a fuller resonance to the idea of relationships.

And it occurred to me: *the Trinity explains this.*

While each Person who makes up the Triune God is equally and fully God, we see how each fulfills a distinct role in the Godhead and in the world. According to the Bible, the Father, the Son, and the Holy Spirit each share the fullness of deity. None of them is *less God* than any other. Each of the three divine Persons is fully and equally God. And yet within the Trinity there appears to be a distribution of function that each divine Person willingly and gladly embraces for the Trinity's own glory and the good of the world. For instance, the Son, while equal to the Father, nevertheless submits to the will of the Father. As we see in Jesus's prayer in John 17, the Son is seeking to glorify the Father. Jesus speaks frequently of doing his

Father's will, of being sent by the Father. Similarly, when Jesus is resurrected he promises to send the Holy Spirit. After his ascension, the Spirit then descends and sets about glorifying the work of the Son, which glorifies the Father.

Each Person of the Trinity fulfills a distinct role that culminates in the unified mission of the Triune God. The Son works to fulfill the Father's vision. The Spirit works to point toward the Son. Each glorifies the others. Some have called this a divine dance. The three Persons with distinct roles share the same divine essence, making up the unified and harmonized one God.

But what we also see in this picture is not just the Trinitarian relationship (three connected to each other) but a Trinitarian community (three in collaboration with each other). We see this collaboration in the work of salvation itself (1 Pet. 1:2). The God who is a community saves us into community. Professor Bruce Ware writes:

> The very fact that God, though singular in nature, is plural and societal in person, indicates that we should not view ourselves as isolated individuals who happen to exist in close proximity to others, but as interconnected, interdependent relational persons in community.[4]

Similarly, the billions of people in the world who have trusted in Jesus Christ operate in distinct roles of varying visibility or authority but share the equality of being God's image-bearers, making up the unified and harmonized body of Christ. As multiple persons (three) make up one God,

4. Bruce A. Ware, *Father, Son, and Holy Spirit: Relationships, Roles, and Relevance* (Wheaton, IL: Crossway, 2005), 134.

multiple people (billions throughout history) make up one church. The apostle Paul speaks of this community this way:

> But as it is, God arranged the members in the body, each one of them, as he chose. If all were a single member, where would the body be? As it is, there are many parts, yet one body. (1 Cor. 12:18–20)

The mission of Jesus isn't simply to reconcile us as individuals to God but also to each other. The mission of Jesus is to make a community.

In doing so, God redeems the very idea of community, which since the fall cannot seem to get its act together. We have tried various governments and philosophies and programs. We have tried tight borders and no borders. But we can't seem to create heaven on earth. There's a reason why the word *utopia* comes from a fable. All of our attempts at orchestrating community cannot keep our self-interest at bay. The vast injustice in the world—in everything from slavery to racism—is the result of our failure at community. Sin messes up our souls; sin messes up our societies.

This is why compartmentalization within the Christian church along racial, social, or gender lines is antithetical to the spirit of God and "against the grain" of the gospel of Jesus Christ. This kind of societal fracture and gathering according to kind is the result of the fall; the unifying of different kinds of people around the grace of God is a sign of God's work in the world.

We like the idea of living in a community where everyone plays a role according to their own gifts and talents, all in mutual admiration and respect of each other, working diversely yet in unity toward a common goal. That's the communal ideal the Trinity perfectly reveals.

The community that the gospel makes, the church, is as fraught with sin as any other community this side of heaven, but as male and female, young and old, black and white, and every shade and stage between focus on their mutual need for God and their mutual acceptance by God, they reflect the Trinity like no other community can.

The Bible teaches that all have sinned and fallen short of the glory of God; therefore, nobody can claim moral superiority. The Bible teaches that anyone who is saved has been saved by the grace of God, not by any personal merit; therefore, nobody has any right to prideful arrogance. The gospel creates a community through the humility of our sin and the loving forgiveness available in Jesus. As Miroslav Volf says, "The relations between the many in the church must reflect the mutual *love* of the divine persons."[5]

The Trinity Personifies Love

"The Beatles said all you need is love," Larry Norman sang. "Then they broke up."

Love is the thing we all know we need. And yet love is the thing we struggle so much to get right. We think of it largely in terms of feelings, of "being in love" or "falling in love," but feelings are fleeting. That kind of love certainly can't be all we need; it is so hard to maintain!

5. Miroslav Volf, *After Our Likeness: The Church as the Image of the Trinity* (Grand Rapids: Eerdmans, 1998), 195 (italics original).

I remember some of the best love advice I ever got. It was right before my wedding, and my dad had taken me aside to encourage me and pray for me. I jokingly said to him, "What if I fall out of love?" He returned my sarcasm, saying, "Then you fall right back in!"

My dad was really making the point that real love is not something you fall in and out of. It is intentional. It has movement. I think of this every time I'm attending a wedding and 1 Corinthians 13 is read. Many couples automatically go to this great "love chapter" in the Bible simply because it's all about love. But I don't think many are paying much attention to what it actually says. Because when things start getting difficult, when conflict pops up—as it inevitably must in close relationships—suddenly keeping no record of wrongs and hoping and bearing all things doesn't seem to make much sense.

The kind of love that is real love, the kind of love the Bible actually teaches, the love that is higher and deeper and stronger than all our stupid pop songs and romance novels and chick flicks is impossible to manufacture out of emotions and human ambition.

So how do we get it?

The religious person will suggest that love comes from God. But Christianity teaches that God is himself love (1 John 4:8, 16).

Love is not God. But God is love. So what does it mean for God to be love?

It does not necessarily mean that God is simply *loving*. Judaism and Islam and Mormonism teach a God who loves. But when Christians teach that God *is himself love*, they are saying that real love itself has its origin and its essence in God. *And this cannot be true unless God is a Trinity.*

Think about it: A solitary god cannot be love. He may learn to love. He may yearn for love. But he cannot in himself be love, because love requires an object. Real love requires relationship. In the doctrine of the Trinity we finally see how love is part of the fabric of creation; it is essential to the eternal, need-nothing Creator. From eternity past, the Father and the Son and the Holy Spirit have been in community, in relationship. They have loved each other. That loving relationship is bound up in the very nature of God himself. If God were not a Trinity but merely a solitary divinity, he could neither be love nor be God!

So the Trinity is not some weird religious aberration Christians have stupidly clung to. It is the answer to the deepest longing of the human heart. The Trinity answers history's oldest desire. It even clarifies the question. It makes us go deeper than sentimental notions and ethereal feelings and elusive emotions. It puts us on solid ground with all this love stuff we've been chasing forever.

"Ultimate reality," Tim Keller says, "is a community of persons who know and love one another. That is what the universe, God, history, and life is all about."[6]

I hope you can see why the Trinity is compelling. I hope you've seen why Christians find it necessary to believe in the Trinity, certainly, but I also hope you will see why we find it not just intellectually convincing but spiritually and emotionally transformative.

6. Timothy Keller, *The Reason for God: Belief in an Age of Skepticism* (New York: Riverhead Books, 2008), 226.

We're all looking for love. Deep down we all need love in ways we don't understand or even acknowledge. We search and search. We find glimpses, moments, tastes, and samples of love. We have genuine experiences of love. And yet nothing quite gets us outside of our own hurts, our own self-interest, our own sins. We need the realest love there is.

Jesus says, "Greater love has no one than this, that someone lay down his life for his friends" (John 15:13). Sacrificial love is the ultimate love.

Now imagine that the One who is Love himself sacrificed himself. Imagine that the eternal loving fellowship of the divine community sent out one of their own to die not just for their friends but for enemies! Why would this loving fellowship do this? To make the enemies friends, of course.

And this is precisely what God has done. The second Person of the Trinity, the Son of God, takes on flesh and comes to die, that he who is true Love might show true love and give true love and transform by true love. That we might finally know true love. It's for this reason that Fred Sanders declares, "Trinity and the gospel have the same shape! This is because the good news of salvation is ultimately that God opens his Trinitarian life to us."[7]

This is the hope of all mankind—that the "fusty doctrine" of the Trinity would "come to life" by swallowing us up into the love God has enjoyed since before time began. C. S. Lewis, who was once himself an atheist, was right

7. Fred Sanders, *The Deep Things of God: How the Trinity Changes Everything* (Wheaton, IL: Crossway, 2010), 98.

when he said, "The thing that matters is being actually drawn into that three-personal life."[8]

And when somebody trusts in the Jesus Christ of Christianity, they are.

8. C. S. Lewis, *Mere Christianity* (Westwood, NJ: Barbour, 1952), 139.

+   +   +   +   **3**   +

Sacred Mirrors

HOW THE CHRISTIAN VIEW OF HUMANITY IS THE MOST OPTIMISTIC

One of my favorite destinations on social media is the Instagram account called "Humans of New York." Every day random people on the streets of New York City are profiled, typically with a quote or two from them that gives a glimpse into their life story. What I love about it is how human it makes these strangers seem.

Their stories help us see beyond stereotypes and preconceived notions. The kid in baggy jeans and grimy tank top we might try to avoid on the sidewalk is coming home from the landscaping job he's working to put himself through law school. The tired woman on the bus who smells a little funny has been working two jobs in fast-food places throughout the week to provide for her disabled husband. It is not an understatement to say that these profiles help us judge more slowly and think the best more quickly.

Everybody has a story. And learning these stories helps us see the way God is working in the world, and the way God is calling out to humanity to understand his care and concern for them.

On the flipside of "Humans of New York" is another social media account I follow, a page on Facebook dedicated to criminal updates in the second largest city in the state I used to live in, Rutland, Vermont. The anonymous administrator of the page keeps an ear connected to the police scanner and relies on tips from subscribers on the streets to help post regularly on arrests, citations, and court verdicts.

Now, Vermont has an interesting reputation as being one of the most liberal states in the nation. It was one of the first to legalize gay marriage. Those who have more recently moved to the state tend to pride themselves on their tolerance. Those who are natives of the state tend to very much fall into the "live and let live" school of societal thought. Vermont is a very peaceful place, a very "nice" place. But you wouldn't know this if you follow this Rutland criminal spotlight page. Drug arrest after drug arrest, within which might be a hundred different stories affecting parents and children and friends and others, get summed up quite tidily in little judgmental bows. The tolerant folk of Vermont on this page left comments like these after a recent update:

"We should shoot this human garbage."

"Kill all these addicts. It's the only way to save the state."

"What a piece of ———."

Don't sound very tolerant, do they?

Now, of course, I know these sorts of comments are par for the internet course. There is a reason there is another social media account (on Twitter) called "Don't Read the Comments." And while I am angry about what heroin is doing to Vermont—and other states—and while I am a supporter of both recovery programs and criminal justice, there is something quite telling any time we find one human being calling another human being a "monster," an "animal," "garbage," or some other expletive.

And I'm going to go out on a limb and say that even many people who think human beings evolved from animals (which evolved originally from some kind of primordial goop) would agree we should not treat humans as animals (or garbage).

But the reality is that we do. And the reality is that this kind of treatment is completely logical if you *do* think people evolved from goop. I mean, even if you can acknowledge that human beings are extraordinary creatures, full of mystery and wonder, brimming with all kinds of untapped potential and genius, if you think we are simply well-ordered animals resulting from happenstance, then thinking of other people as animals is not far out of hand. And then treating other people as animals is not much further.

The Christian view of humanity is another thing entirely. I want to admit up front that too many Christians throughout history have royally screwed this up. There have been too many prominent examples of professing Christians treating others as less-than-human. This is wrong. And we believe God will judge this. But when someone claiming to be a Christian treats another human being poorly, it is because he or she is, at least in that moment, functionally disbelieving what the Bible says about human beings—that they are made in the image of God and thus are *sacred*.

People Are Beautiful, Even When They're Not "Useful"

Every person has a story. And one of the great things about "Humans of New York" is not just that it gives you the narrative of the souls we might be tempted to avoid on the street but of the souls we might not even notice. Every single person you pass by, whether they catch your eye or not, is incredibly interesting.

But I want to argue, actually, that while many people can agree that every person is interesting, only biblical Christianity treats all human life as *sacred*. This will seem difficult to prove, because there is so much said by so many traditions, both religious and irreligious, that speaks to the significance of all people, to the need for more love in the world, and to the systemic injustice in many cultures. But if we dig a little deeper than the rhetoric, I think we will find many of these sentiments somewhat selective in their application.

The commenters on that Rutland crime page, for instance, probably treat their families well. They probably show general kindness to those they meet on a day-to-day basis. But when it comes to drug addicts, there seems to be no punishment too severe.

Similarly, I find it completely illogical that any person or organization can claim to support justice and human rights while maintaining a woman's right to abort her baby. Human rights, it seems, only apply to a certain subset of humanity, not to all humans.

The way most people in the world sort through who gets to be treated well and who gets to be treated like animals usually corresponds to some set of what we might call "utilitarian values." People are thought to have a basic utility. They are found useful or not useful and then treated accordingly. The person who believes women should have a right to end the lives of their unborn children does so based on the idea that children may be an undue burden, that they may be inconvenient or a hardship of some kind. And of course all children are burdens and hardships! They require constant supervision and nurturing.

Others make similar arguments about the very old or the very disabled. It seems that quite regularly our national conversation gets taken over by questions of euthanasia and physician-assisted suicide. These issues are incredibly complex, but at their basis lies a fundamental idea: the value of life is contingent on its ease or comfort.

In the religious world, utilitarian values compel people toward discrimination, injustice, fanaticism, and even terrorism. When some religious groups are convinced the objects of their mission will not convert to their way of thinking, they become expendable. Sometimes they become victims of violence. We definitely see this playing out in portions of the Middle East, where certain forms of Islam are becoming dominant not by converting unbelievers but by killing them.

These utilitarian values are not absent from the evangelical Christian world. They pop up in a variety of ways. One of the instances that bugs me most is in the abortion discussion. You have likely heard this line of reasoning from earnest pro-lifers before: "You should be pro-life because you never know if you've aborted the next Einstein, the next Beethoven, the next Martin Luther King Jr., the next Pasteur or Salk, etc." I mean, what if you aborted the curer of cancer or of AIDS?

The motivation behind these kinds of statements is understandable, and the underlying reasoning is sound: abortion, which does immediate, seen harm to unborn children and many of their mothers, also does unseen future harm to families, communities, and the world.

But I hate this argument against abortion and here's why: it assigns value based on (presumed) accomplishments. It is a utilitarian argument—assigning intrinsic value based on one's "utility"—and utilitarian arguments are best suited for pro-choice arguments, not pro-life. Those seeking abortions are already employing utilitarianism in their thinking. For example: "This child will have a poor life, so it is best to prevent him or her from experiencing it," or "This child will interfere with my plans for the future, so it is best to terminate my pregnancy until I am really ready."

This reasoning also fails to consider that we are actually right now perilously close to abortion based on predictive value. In America, it is dangerous to be an unborn African American. In China, it is dangerous to be an unborn girl. As fertility treatments become more advanced, parents have potential to someday "custom design" their babies, right down to hair and eye color. What would be done, then, with "error" babies? They could be thrown away like garbage. And of course abortions of unborn children with Down syndrome and other conditions that seem disagreeable to their prospective parents are commonplace already. What happens in the day when technology can show us that a child will be mentally advanced? What happens to the mentally "just average" fetuses then? Some are asking gay rights advocates if they would remain pro-choice if in the future that elusive "gay gene" they keep searching for could be found? What if moms wanted to abort their babies for fear they'd be gay?

No, the utilitarian view of human life has no place in the Christian worldview, and evangelicals should give it no place in their efforts against abortion, as powerful or convicting as those arguments might seem to be.

The biblical grounds for the sacredness of human life have nothing to do with a person's "usefulness" to a family or society. The Bible calls us to the pro-life position based on the reality that all persons are made in the image of God, that God has created us equal, and that therefore all life is precious, whether a person cures cancer or gets cancer, wins an Olympic medal or a Special Olympics medal, can compose like Mozart or sings like Roseanne Barr.

Suppose we could save the future Einsteins and Beethovens from the abortionist. It would still be just as tragic and just as sinful to have otherwise commenced with the offing of future stay-at-home moms, truck mechanics, and janitors. You know, all the "ordinary people" of which there are so many more than the so-called extraordinary people.

The Christian view of humanity would argue, in fact, that abortion is wrong whether you happen to be aborting the next Mother Teresa or the next Adolf Hitler. Christians don't even believe that Christian lives are more important than non-Christian lives. In fact, a biblically minded Christian would think that giving up his or her own life to save that of an unbeliever would be better, because living another day gives that unbeliever another day in which he or she might come to know God.

So if Christians, unlike other religions and traditions, do not base their view of the sacredness of life on some kind of usefulness, what do they base it on?

All Life Is Sacred

"So God created man in his own image, in the image of God he created him; male and female he created them." This revelation, found in Genesis 1:27, is the profoundest basis for human exceptionality one could hope to find. Human life isn't sacred because we managed to be the experiment of nature that finally worked. Human life isn't sacred because we are beneficial to each other or to society. Human life isn't sacred when it is wanted or desired or loved. Human life is sacred because God created it *in his own image*.

We aren't sure what this rightly means. For humankind to be made in God's image may relate to the way our body, mind, and spirit reflect God's Triune nature. It may relate to the fact that we are conscious of our existence in ways animals are not. It may refer to the fact that we have souls in ways animals do not, souls that may enjoy communion with God himself. We may not ever understand the depths of what it means to be made in God's image, precisely because it is a very weighty, profound thing. But Christians believe that human life is sacred because God has created humanity to be his image-bearers, and it is a terrible thing to exploit or destroy an image-bearer.

God has given us all sorts of clues, even within our own bodies, to lead us to this conclusion. Sometimes he even has the weakest and most vulnerable among us remind us in dramatic ways. Perhaps you have seen the rather dramatic photograph of a tiny hand reaching out from an open womb and grasping the finger of a surgeon. The story behind the image is remarkable.

Julie and Alex Armas struggled for a long time trying to have children, and after two miscarriages eventually conceived once more. But it wasn't too far into the pregnancy that problems began occurring. Agonizing cramps prompted an ultrasound, which revealed that Julie and Alex's baby was not developing properly. Their unborn child was diagnosed with spina bifida.

Doctors advised an abortion. The Armases refused. But the prospect of raising a disabled child was still nerve-wracking. Alex said they felt "torn apart."[1]

Motivation to research their baby's condition and any available help, however, led them to a team at Vanderbilt University in Nashville, Tennessee, where they qualified for an experimental surgery conducted *in utero* on the baby's spinal cord. If done early enough, it could offset much of the damage promised by spina bifida.

The surgery was controversial and risky. Because medical science did not have any way to keep a twenty-one-week-old fetus alive outside the womb, everything must go according to plan. And the risks to Julie were just as great.

> Finally the day arrived. During the surgery, Dr. Bruner could be heard urging his team to keep quiet. "Shh!" he said. "You'll wake the baby!"
>
> Robert Davis, who reported on the operation for *USA Today*, said the lesion that exposed Samuel's spine was found low on his backbone, decreasing the chance of nerve damage.
>
> Although Samuel is believed to have been the youngest patient for such an operation, it was apparently routine enough for Dr. Bruner and pediatric neurosurgeon Noel Tullpant to talk about the weather during the operation.[2]

But everyone has a story to tell:

> As the surgeon was closing the womb, the miracle happened. Unborn Samuel Armas pushed his hand out of the

1. "Holding Hands," *Independent* (October 30, 1999), http://www.independent.ie/irish-news/holding-hands-26136931.html.
2. Ibid.

womb and grabbed the surgeon's finger. Photographer Michael Clancy caught this astonishing act on film. And in that instant, Clancy went from being prochoice to being prolife. As he put it, "I was totally in shock for two hours after the surgery. . . . I know abortion is wrong now—it's absolutely wrong."[3]

Baby Samuel wanted to remind everyone that all human life is sacred. Reaching out of his mother's womb to hold the hand of his surgeon, he was putting an exclamation point on Psalm 139:13–16:

> For you formed my inward parts;
> > you knitted me together in my mother's womb.
> I praise you, for I am fearfully and wonderfully
> > made.
> > Wonderful are your works;
> > my soul knows it very well.
> > My frame was not hidden from you,
> when I was being made in secret,
> > intricately woven in the depths of the earth.
> Your eyes saw my unformed substance;
> in your book were written, every one of them,
> > the days that were formed for me,
> > when as yet there was none of them.

This is why Christians believe in the sacredness of human life—because God has made humankind his image-bearers, and whatever this means, it cannot mean because humankind is "useful," but *beautiful*.

3. Quoted in John Piper, "God at Work in Every Womb," *Desiring God* (January 21, 2001), http://www.desiringgod.org/sermons/god-at-work-in-every-womb.

Humans are the only creatures that ponder. Not just think, but ponder. No animal looks up at the moon and wants to go see what's there. No animal muses on the meaning of life, feels existential angst or dread, or experiences the pure joy of thinking beautiful things. Animals make beautiful things, for sure, but they always have utility. Only humans make art, which serves no useful benefit except to our souls, to make our hearts sing or think or wonder. No animal explores simply for the sake of exploration, to see what's around the corner, to see new things and exult in them.

We are not just glorified animals. We are reflections of God, sacred mirrors. All of us. Which is why the Christian concept of justice is the most logical concept of justice in the world. It is predicated not on someone's usefulness to society but on God's image implanted in their very being.

These Are the People in Your Neighborhood

What Christians believe about the sacredness of human life, then, has direct ramifications on what they believe about society. We will explore this theme a little more fully when we talk about Christian mission, but it is important to mention now, because biblically speaking, Christianity is not an individualistic faith. Christians have a personal relationship with God, but it is not meant to be a *private* relationship with God.

Christians believe that Jesus Christ, in fulfilling the Hebrew Scriptures' predictions of God coming to rescue and redeem Israel, ushered in the kingdom of God through his own ministry, culminating with his death and resurrection. When Jesus came to do this, the ways of God were declared to people outside the nation of Israel, to every tongue, tribe, race, and nation, that they may be included in the relationship with God made possible through Jesus. The way the Old Testament speaks to this coming kingdom has heavy overtones of justice. It speaks not just to the ways we treat each other as individuals but to the ways God is working in the world among cultures and nations.

When God made Adam and Eve in his image, he gave them the mandate to build and create and cultivate, to nurture and nourish civilization. Beginning with a garden, God gave them the mission to establish a city where he himself was the glorious center. When they disobeyed God and sin entered the world—more on this in the next chapter—it wasn't just their own souls that got bent inward but also their mission. What you see in the ensuing pages of Genesis is a long history of injustice, warfare, and oppression. Without God at the center, human beings cannot figure out how to live in harmony.

But the calling to seek peace and justice is still there. And it is rooted fundamentally in the call to see our fellow human beings—our *neighbors*, to use the biblical term—as sacred souls made in the image of God.

The prophet Jeremiah tells us a Word of the Lord that gives us an eternal perspective about personhood. "Before I formed you in the womb I knew you, and before you were born I consecrated you; I appointed you a prophet to the nations" (Jer. 1:5). Humans are sacred not just at biological conception but at divine conception, when God first thinks of them.

And this has huge implications for justice and societal harmony in the Hebrew Scriptures. We certainly see this in the books of the law, where numerous commands are given regarding the treatment of foreigners, servants, and the like. But we also see it in the ponderings of righteous men like Job. Take a look at this reflection from perhaps history's most famous sufferer:

> If I have rejected the cause of my manservant or
> my maidservant,
> when they brought a complaint against me,
> what then shall I do when God rises up?
> When he makes inquiry, what shall I answer
> him?
> Did not he who made me in the womb make him?
> And did not one fashion us in the womb? (Job
> 31:13–15)

It is worth mentioning that Job did not live in a time when wealthy people tended to treat their servants with much dignity. Servants and slaves were far too often regarded as "less-than-persons." But despite this, Job's remarks are very telling. I note three important things about humanity in this passage. First, the basis of civil equality is traced to the womb. The well-to-do Job acknowledges that he is equal in personhood to his servants. He grounds this assertion in their equal status as unborn children.

Second, the development of the unborn is a work of God. Job talks about being made and fashioned in the womb by God himself. Third, but not last, what Job is saying here tells us that the treatment of persons as non-persons is something for which we will give an account to God. At the day of judgment, when we are faced with the billions of unborn children who have been murdered for the sake of convenience or fear, "What then shall we do?" When God rises up to ask us to give an account for our ambivalent response to human trafficking, to the sex trade, to pornography and adultery and countless other variations of sexual objectification, to the marginalization of the elderly and the disabled and the poor, to racism and discrimination, what shall we answer him?

It is biblical thinking like this that drove the consistent Christianity of the abolitionist movement against the unjust work of the inconsistent Christian institutions thriving on slavery. It is biblical thinking like this that drives the new pro-life advocacy, that reaches beyond simplistic anti-abortion rhetoric and toward the alleviation of poverty and the rapid growth of adoption in the United States and beyond.

Job 31:13–15 tells us that all people were formed by God in the womb, and because we know all people are made in God's image, we know people have equal claim to personhood, both inside the womb and out.

Now, you may rightly point out that this passage, as well as those from Psalms and Jeremiah, are found in the Jewish canon. I will not argue that Christians and Jews do not share this heritage of human rights. I will only point out two things: I find it odd that, by and large, outside the minority view of orthodox Judaism, most streams of mainstream Judaism tend to align with a pro-choice world-view, at least as it pertains to abortion.

Christianity, however, makes its departure and gains its momentum in the revelation in the New Testament about the kingdom of God hinted at in these Old Testament texts. Once again, we see that the point at which Christianity stands alone in the world of ideas is right at the person of Jesus Christ.

Jesus comes to actualize what the psalmists sing about, Jeremiah preaches about, and Job ruminates about. Jesus comes to develop these thoughts of God into perfect action, commanding us to love our enemies and then actually obeying his own command by dying to forgive people who hate him.

"Love your neighbor as yourself," Jesus says to his followers. And while love is a popular idea in lots of religions and even secular movements, only Jesus Christ had the guts to actually mean it, do it, and die for it.

Christianity, then, looks to Jesus not simply as a good teacher or wise leader but as the perfection of humanity. Once again, Christianity remains unparalleled as a religion thanks to the uniqueness of Jesus Christ.

The Perfect Mirror

Do you ever wonder where love comes from?

If the atheists are right, love is in large part sort of a trick our chemistry plays on us. It is simply a feeling generated by attachment or conditioning or evolutionary expediency. Imagine a child running up to his or her mother and crying out, "Mommy, I love you!" What would you think of the mother who responded, "Yes, I feel a release of serotonin in conditioned biological response to my familial attachment to you, as well"? I have a friend who on Facebook always tells people "Happy Birthday" by posting, "Congratulations on the completion of your gestation!" The point of the joke is to sort of take the romance out of the whole event, isn't it?

It's in religion that we learn that love comes from somewhere. Not from the right firing of the chemical lightning in the biological matrix of our genes, not from the conditioned response to social attachments and the furtherance of the species but from a kind of outer space, from outside of ourselves, from a place like heaven, actually. Most religious people believe love comes from outside of humans and is put inside of them. There are a variety of feelings about this. The monotheistic religions believe that love in some way comes from God.

Only Christianity believes that the one God is a community of three Persons who eternally and coequally love each other so much that this love had to overspill the bounds of their perfect relationship into the world they created to reflect their own love. And only Christianity believes that Jesus Christ was the Son of God, come to embody this love of God in the flesh and love his neighbors and love his Father perfectly, that he might bridge the gap created by sin between humankind and the Father, that humankind might have the Father's love and that the Father might be loved by humankind.

I feel a little breathless just writing that! And I think that's kind of the point. I don't think it's right to talk about love in dispassionate, disconnected ways. Christians believe that humans love because God has put the capacity to know and give love inside of them. "We love because he first loved us" (1 John 4:19).

We are made in the image of God, but Jesus Christ is the perfect image of God (Col. 1:15). This is not only unparalleled among religious worldviews but also offensive to many of them. But biblical Christianity will not shy away from this truth, because we know love that never lets us down, love that will forgive us forever, love that will sustain us and secure us and satisfy us, the kind of perfect love that is described in 1 Corinthians 13, must come from someone who is perfect. And only Jesus Christ fits the bill, because only God is perfect.

If you are compelled to love in a truly sacrificial way but find yourself balking at the truth claims of Christianity, I would urge you not to put down your philosophical musings and logical reasoning but rather to add alongside them a focus on the person and work of Jesus Christ. Because I believe that if God is calling you through Jesus, you will find your arguments answered in the meanwhile. I love this testimony from Dr. Francis Collins, one of the world's foremost scientists and a former atheist:

> I grew up in a home where faith was not an important part of my experience. And when I got to college and people began discussing late at night in the dorm whether God exists, there were lots of challenges to that idea, and I decided I had no need for that . . . . [A]s I got more into this reductionist mode of thinking that characterizes a lot of the physical and biological sciences, it was even more

attractive to just dismiss the concept of anything outside of the natural world.

At one point, one of my patients challenged me, asking me what I believed, and I realized, as I stammered out something about "I don't believe any of this," that it all sounded rather thin in the face of this person's clearly very strong, dedicated belief in God. . . . I decided I'd better investigate this thing called faith so that I could shoot it down more effectively and not have another one of those awkward moments . . .

[I knocked] on the door of a Methodist minister who lived down the street and asked him if he could make any recommendations for somebody who, like me, was looking for some arguments for or against faith. He took a book off his shelf—*Mere Christianity* by C. S. Lewis. Lewis had been an atheist [and] set out as I did to convince himself of the correctness of his position and accidentally converted himself. I took the book home, and in the first few pages realized that all of my arguments in favor of atheism were quickly reduced to rubble by the simple logic of this clear-thinking Oxford scholar. I realized, "I've got to start over again here. Everything that I had based my position upon is really flawed to the core."[4]

What's interesting is that this man did not then abandon science. It is not as if becoming a believer in Jesus meant losing his mind. But it meant that what he was finding in his scientific pursuits was not answering the deepest cries of his heart; meanwhile, what his ailing patients possessed

4. David Ian Miller, "Finding My Religion: Leader of the Human Genome Project Argues in a New Book That Science and Religion Can Coexist Happily," *San Francisco Gate* (August 7, 2006), http://www.sfgate.com/news/article /FINDING-MY-RELIGION-Leader-of-the-Human-Genome-3299361.php.

did. In the end, he still had his science, still had his logic and his reason. But he also discovered that materialism could not produce the kind of enduring love that comes from outside of us, the kind that comes from heaven.

Nancy Pearcey shares her story of conversion this way:

> While still at L'Abri, I had once accosted another student, demanding that he explain why he had converted to Christianity. A pale, thin young man with a strong South African accent, he responded simply, "They shot down all my arguments."
>
> I continued gazing at him somewhat quizzically, expecting something more, well, dramatic. "It's not always a big emotional experience, you know," he said with an apologetic smile. "I just came to see that a better case could be made for Christianity than for any of the other ideas I came here with." It was the first time I had encountered someone whose conversion had been strictly intellectual, and little did I know at the time that my own conversion would be similar.
>
> Back in the States, as I tested out Schaeffer's ideas in the classroom, I was also reading works by C. S. Lewis, G. K. Chesterton, Os Guinness, James Sire, and other apologists. But inwardly, I also had a young person's hunger for reality, and one day I picked up David Wilkerson's *The Cross and the Switchblade*. Now, here was a story exciting enough to suit anyone's taste for the dramatic—stories of Christians braving the slums and witnessing supernatural healings from drug addiction. Fired up with the hope that maybe God would do something equally spectacular in my own life, that night I begged Him, if He was real, to perform some supernatural sign for me—promising that if He did,

I would believe in Him. Thinking that maybe this sort of thing worked better with an aggressive approach, I vowed to stay up all night until He gave me a sign.

Midnight passed, then one o'clock, two o'clock, four o'clock . . . my eyes were closing in spite of myself, and still no spectacular sign had appeared. Finally, rather chagrined about engaging in such theatrics, I abandoned the vigil. And as I did, suddenly I found myself speaking to God simply and directly from the depths of my spirit, with a profound sense of His presence. I acknowledged that I did not really need external signs and wonders because, in my heart of hearts, I had to admit (rather ruefully) that I was already convinced that Christianity was true. Through the discussions at L'Abri and my readings in apologetics, I had come to realize there were good and sufficient arguments against moral relativism, physical determinism, epistemological subjectivism, and a host of other isms I had been carrying around in my head. As my South African friend had put it, all my own ideas had been shot down. The only step that remained was to acknowledge that I had been persuaded—and then give my life to the Lord of Truth.

So, at about four-thirty that morning, I quietly admitted that God had won the argument.[5]

God has won the argument, and he will use any means to do so, including the intellect. Because he created it! He certainly can win souls through it. But in the end, even those who come to faith through these kinds of means are finding something more than simply an intellectual satisfaction. They are finding their souls satisfied.

5. Nancy Pearcey, *Total Truth* (Wheaton, IL: Crossway, 2004), 54–55. Reprinted by permission.

Maybe God is calling you too. Maybe you've got good arguments against trusting in Jesus. But if he is wooing you, I think you will find these arguments answered. In the meantime, his love is calling you. If you were to face him honestly, you would see, I think, that there is no single person ever to live like Jesus Christ. Simply considering the things he said and did will prove this. And in the end, he didn't come to win the argument but to win *you*.

One of the arguments you might have, in fact, is that the Christians around you seem to do a lousy job of embodying this stuff like Jesus did. It was Gandhi who famously said, "I very much like your Christ. But your Christ is so different from your Christians."

I don't exactly think this is true. But he did have a point.

And as you can imagine, Christians themselves have in their own unique truth claims a very good explanation for this.

4

Broken Mirrors

HOW THE CHRISTIAN VIEW OF HUMANITY IS THE MOST REALISTIC

I used to work in building maintenance with a guy who was extremely nice to me, despite having no reason to be. He was technically my boss, but he treated me like a peer and colleague. While I was just passing time trying to earn some money while training for vocational ministry, he'd been doing construction and maintenance-type work for years, with no hope or even aspiration to move beyond it. In his own estimation, I was a white collar guy slumming in the blue collar world, which was his environment. Yet he never treated me like I was unwelcome, never looked at me with contempt. He was always asking me theological questions and seeking my advice on relationship matters, trusting that I'd provide the kind of counsel a good religious man would.

This guy was exceedingly kind to me. He gave me ample time off, didn't micromanage me, didn't second guess, didn't sneer when my very obvious lack of "being handy" made it laughable that I was working maintenance. He was constantly taking heat for things I failed to do when he wasn't fixing things I had incompetently repaired.

You might be surprised to know that this guy was also kind of a deadbeat when it came to providing for his ex-wife. He was frequently in legal trouble for not providing spousal support. I don't think this failure was due to lack of money, because he was always bragging about fixing up a beach house he'd purchased or showing off upgrades he'd been making to his new pickup truck. He also couldn't seem to stay out of jail, for all kinds of reasons, mostly related to drug offenses, DUIs, driving without a license, petty theft, and other things.

I have no excuses for these things. How he lived in relation to his ex-wife and to the world was incredibly wrong. And yet he was one of the best bosses I've ever had.

How can this be?

As my friend Ray Ortlund says, "We are not balanced persons."

It probably does not surprise you to know that the same people who believe that Jesus Christ is both fully God and fully man can also believe that human beings are both profoundly sacred and profoundly broken. These two truth claims do not seem to go together. Christians believe that the Bible teaches that men and women are made in God's image but that men and women are also desperately wicked. We have, at the same time, an incredibly optimistic view of the world and an incredibly pessimistic view of the world.

In fact, when those who claim to be Christians go wrong in their treatment of people, it is usually because they have not quite figured out how to hold these equally important truths in tension. When people believe that human beings are only desperately wicked but do not acknowledge that they are made in God's image and thus sacred, they trend toward objectification, judgmentalism, and hatred. I do not believe the group that calls themselves Westboro Baptist Church are genuine believers in Jesus Christ, but they would be one example of a religious group that affirms the Bible's teaching on sin but rejects the Bible's teaching on love. They do not treat their enemies like people made in God's image.

On the flip side, so much of what we see in the so-called progressive Christian circles—what used to be called the emergent church and is really just the shallow end of the mainline Protestant tradition—affirms that people are sacred and made in God's image but waffles on the sinfulness of humanity, which often leads them to affirm behaviors the Bible condemns and endorse beliefs the Bible denies.

I do think that evangelicals are beginning to figure out this tension. We have not done a great job throughout our history. Like all people, we tend to overreact and ride the pendulum of belief from one extreme to another.

Sometimes we find ourselves affirming sacredness to the extent of sinfulness, and sometimes vice versa. I don't think we'll ever get this perfect, but I do think we are improving, and a lot of it is due to the help of people like Russell Moore, head of the Southern Baptist Convention's Ethics and Religious Liberties Commission (ERLC).

I know, I know. Most people don't expect a compassionate worldview for humanity coming from Southern Baptists, much less a Southern Baptist organization dedicated to "religious liberty," a phrase so fraught with difficulty in these days of cultural fallout from the Moral Majority and the right-wing culture wars of the 1980s and '90s. But listen to what Dr. Moore says about one particular issue at the forefront of much societal angst today:

> Ultimately, the transgender question is about more than just sex. It's about what it means to be human.
>
> As conservative Christians, we do not see transgendered persons as "freaks" to be despised or ridiculed. We acknowledge that there are some persons who feel alienated from their identities as men or as women. Of course that would be the case in a fallen universe in which all of us are alienated, in some way, from how God created us to be . . .
>
> [W]e will love and be patient with those who feel alienated from their created identities. We must recognize that some in our churches will face a long road of learning what it means to live as God created them to be, as male or female. That sort of long, slow, plodding and sometimes painful obedience is part of what Jesus said would be true of every believer: the bearing of a cross. That cross-bearing reminds us that God doesn't receive us because of our own

effort but because God reconciled us to himself through the life, death, and resurrection of Jesus . . .

All we can do is say what we believe as Christians: that all of us are sinners, and that none of us are freaks. We must conclude that all of us are called to repentance, and part of what repentance means is to receive the gender with which God created us, even when that's difficult. We must affirm that God loves all persons, and that the gospel is good news for repentant prodigal sons and daughters.[1]

Depending on your viewpoint, it may disappoint you that Moore maintains the biblical view of transgenderism as sexually disordered, or it may disappoint you that he seems too soft on this view. He has taken fire over his tenure at the ERLC from both the religious and the irreligious. In my mind, I think this means he may be on to something.

I notice phrases in this piece like "fallen universe in which all of us are alienated," "painful obedience is part of what Jesus said would be true of every believer," "all of us are sinners," "all of us are called to repentance," and "God loves all persons."

Again, you may find what he's saying about transgenderism deplorable, but you cannot say he isn't lumping *everybody* into the "sexually disordered" category. There is nobody in the history of the universe, save Jesus himself, who was totally sexually normal. We all suffer in some way from sexual sin or disorder. Acknowledging this doesn't

1. Russell D. Moore, "Conservative Christianity and the Transgender Question," *Moore to the Point* (August 12, 2013), http://www.russellmoore.com/2013/08/12/conservative-christianity-and-the-transgender-question/.

make Christians "soft on homosexuality" or "soft on sin." It simply makes them human and reasonable.

I think what Moore does well is hold that difficult tension as inextricable from the Christian view of humanity. We are beautiful, wonderful, sacred creatures. And we are sinful, broken, disobedient rebels.

Glorious and Inglorious

I had just arrived in Orlando, Florida, for a speaking engagement, and being the simple person that I am, I was instantly in awe of the radio in my rental car. I had a long drive from the airport to my first appointment, and I was thrilled to be able to peruse for only the second or third time in my life the technological wonder known as satellite radio.

Have you experienced such a thing?

Well, of course you likely have, but at the time I had lived in Vermont for six years, where more than a few people in my church did not have computers in their home and where I did not even have cellular phone service at the office or at home. I had grown quite accustomed to a low-tech existence—which I quite enjoyed—so when exposed to the miracle of satellite radio I was like Jed Clampett pondering the luxury of indoor plumbing.

Now, what do you think I listened to on this satellite radio? I had an almost endless selection of radio stations. Every click of the dial brought in crystal-clear audio. I love music from the '50s and '60s, and there were entire sections of stations devoted to the great oldies sounds of yesteryear.

I scanned the aural landscape of music, sports, comedy, talk radio, and more, and where do you think I landed?

Well, I am a very strange person indeed, profoundly beautiful in my own way but also desperately wicked, so I tuned in with ironic glee to the preaching of Joel Osteen.

I confess that I often listen to Osteen the same way many people slow down on the highway to get a good lookie-loo at a wreck in the ditch. To the biblical Christian, the kind of moralistic, therapeutic deism one finds in this kind of preaching is the theological version of a car wreck.

But I must also confess that this particular sermon wasn't entirely bad. Osteen appeared to be actually preaching from a biblical text, which is not too common for him, and in this instance was speaking from Matthew 8, where Jesus and his disciples are in a boat at sea in the middle of a storm. The disciples are very afraid, but Jesus commands the storm to cease, and restores peace to both the sea and to the disciples' hearts.

Osteen said some interesting things about this passage. He did not say anything particularly deep or profoundly theological. His points were quite simple and rudimentary, but they weren't entirely wrong. The application he ultimately made was this: we will frequently find ourselves in the midst of storms in our lives, but we need to know that the same power Jesus used to calm the storm is inside of us.

There is a lot of truth to this. As I said, it wasn't entirely wrong. But neither was it entirely right. See, in Osteen's theological world, the worst things people face are outside of themselves, things that might happen to them or, in the spiritual economy of the prosperity gospel, things that might *not* happen to them. Listening to some of this preaching quite frequently—yes, I'm a glutton for punishment—I am struck by how awful they make it seem to not come into riches or perfect health. But the things the Bible says about humanity go much deeper than this. And I don't know about you, but my own experience has proved it true. The worst storms I have faced in my life have not occurred outside of me but rather have been found inside of me.

And I think this is something the Bible consistently calls us to face. Here is something Jesus says that I find incredibly intriguing and, in a way, disturbing: "And do not fear those who kill the body but cannot kill the soul" (Matt. 10:28). In other words, Jesus is saying that dying isn't the worst thing that can happen to you. There are worse things than our bodies dying. What could he be referring to?

He is referring to the very real danger of our souls dying in the great judgment that comes after our bodies die.

You don't have to believe what Jesus is saying here, but you have to understand it to understand Jesus. Don't reject the Jesus you haven't properly considered. Jesus is actually saying that my worst enemy is myself. It's not even death. Because we're all going to die at some point. Nobody gets out alive. But Jesus has promised that if I repent of my sin and trust in him, I will be with him forever in the joy of the kingdom. But if I don't repent and trust in him, I will reap what my sin has sown.

The deepest, most profound evil I will ever face is that which is found inside of me.

Again, you may not believe it, but I urge you to consider it. This is what Christianity teaches. Only in Christianity do we find this necessary tension between human potential for both beauty and evil. And only in Christianity do we find this wonderful tension between what we deserve in our sin and what we win in Christ.

More Sinful Than We Think, More Loved Than We Know

You are worse than you think you are.

Or, I don't know, maybe you're a better person than me, and you either know how bad you are or you actually think you're not that bad.

I like to think I'm a pretty self-aware guy. I am neurotic and messy. I constantly worry about offending people or annoying people, and frequently I find that my worries are well-founded. I also know I do lots of wrong things. I know, I know—a religious guy like me certainly can't be guilty of too much wrong, but when I start making a list I get pretty depressed. Here's a list of some wrong things I did *just today*:

- I woke up later than I planned and so I didn't spend time in the Bible first thing in the morning, as I ought. And then I didn't feel guilty about it. Until now.
- I was on a plane and planned to do some writing on this book but a rather heavyset woman sat next to me and I could not move my left arm freely enough to type, so I lost ninety minutes of writing time. It was inconvenient and frustrating, but my attitude was terrible and I internally judged her for not "taking

care of herself." While scrutinizing her thoughtlessness toward me, I was being incredibly and stupidly thoughtless toward her. Though I don't suppose she knew I felt this way, this is still a huge violation of her sacredness as a human being made in God's image and a disobedience to the call to love my neighbor as myself.

- When I arrived at my destination, I thought about a certain person I hoped would not be there, because I did not want to talk to him.

- At the same event, I relished people's compliments too much.

- I also gossiped about people I don't like.

- In the airport in the evening, tired and bored, I battled too weakly with lust while people-watching.

I am on a flight home right now as I type this list, and if I'm committing any sin at the moment, it's worrying what you will think about me when reading it. I could write more, but my publisher has given me a word limit on this book.

Now, you may have read this brief survey of today's iniquities and think I'm a pretty awful person. But you don't know the half of it!

And I don't either. I like to think I'm pretty self-aware, but I am not even half aware of the sins I commit on a daily basis, especially the internal kinds of sins, the petty thoughts and slights and irritated reactions. I committed so many sins today that I might never see, even with many days' worth of remembering. All of my motives are mixed, all of my "good works" tainted with whiffs of self-interest.

The theologian known as the apostle Paul wrestles with this same problem in Romans 7, when he writes: "For I have the desire to do what is right, but not the ability to carry it out. For I do not do the good I want, but the evil I do not want is what I keep on doing" (vv. 18–19). He finds himself in a very human predicament. There are good things he knows he ought to do, but he cannot find the ability to do them all that well. And then there are bad things he knows he ought not do, but he finds himself constantly doing them over and over again. It's exhausting trying to "be good" all the time, mainly because it's impossible.

In my years of pastoral ministry, I have been regularly surprised by the number of people I'd encounter who seemed to see no conflict at all in their being ridiculously kind in certain spheres of life while being ridiculously petty in others. I frequently dealt with women who gossiped as zealously as they served at charity dinners and men who treated their children warmly while remaining cold and aloof to their wives. Some of the most visibly self-effacing advocates for the pro-life cause outside the church were the harshest and most malicious critics against people inside the church.

I could never quite figure this out. Couldn't they see the discrepancy? How could they not daily feel the weight of their own duplicity?

We are worse than we think we are.

Most irreligious worldviews espouse some form of innate human goodness. This is attributed to all sorts of sources, but in general, most people tend to be optimistic about the human potential for good. It is this worldview, in fact, that has declared a lot of religion bad!

But most religious worldviews also share the sentiment. Every religion deals with human evil in its own particular way, but because every religious system (except for Christianity) suggests that salvation, enlightenment, fulfillment, heaven, or what-have-you is achievable through adherence to a certain set of behaviors, codes, or steps, they all basically affirm some trace of innate goodness in humankind rendering such adherence possible.

Then Christianity comes along and says that not only do we fail to obey God's rules perfectly but we *can't* obey them perfectly.

This sounds like a huge bummer, and in a way it certainly is. But it's also, to my mind, surprisingly refreshing. Because the more I think about it, the more this pessimistic view of humanity actually seems to make the most sense of humanity.

We do have a great capacity for goodness and for beauty and for endurance. But then terrible things keep happening in the world, and we can't quite figure out where they've come from. They don't seem to fit with how we think the world should be (because they don't), but we can't quite figure out how to get the world ordered in the right way to prevent these things.

So we try all sorts of social experiments. Communes and communism. Free markets and free love. State religion and no religion. Less laws and more laws. We try to socially engineer our way out of the pervasive problem of human evil, but we can't do it.

We are worse than we think we are.

We should be thankful, then, that the Bible comes along and shoots straight with us. Because it doesn't only reveal that people sin. We probably wouldn't need it just to tell us that. The evidence is pretty clear. The Bible goes further, and tells us sin is inside of us and corrupts everything we think, say, and do. And in fact, it's even worse than *that*. Paul later writes this in the New Testament:

> And you were dead in the trespasses and sins in which you once walked, following the course of this world, following the prince of the power of the air, the spirit that is now at work in the sons of disobedience—among whom we all once lived in the passions of our flesh, carrying out the desires of the body and the mind, and were by nature children of wrath, like the rest of mankind. (Eph. 2:1–3)

Things don't look very good for us.

Ephesians 2 is one of those passages in the Bible that shows us the bigness, the majesty, the absolute sovereignty of God. But one of the ways it does this is by revealing the contrast of human deficiency. Only the great light of God could cast such a big shadow. And the shadow is *huge*.

It was sociologist Christian Smith who diagnosed the prevailing message of nominal Christianity and other pop religions as "moralistic therapeutic deism." The gist of this superficial spirituality is that people are simply disabled; they need a spiritual "leg up." But this is not the picture in Ephesians 2. No, Paul is devastatingly clear when he says that people apart from Jesus Christ are:

Dead.

Devil-followers.

Appetite-driven.

Children of wrath.

You may likely object to at least a few of these claims. (You will probably balk at being called a devil-worshiper, especially if it's been a while since you listened to the band Slayer or whatever.) But let's take it step by step to at least see the logic behind the claims.

When Paul says that apart from Christ living inside of us we are dead, he doesn't mean that we don't exercise our wills or that we aren't conscious or that our choices aren't real. He simply means that, spiritually speaking, if we do not desire God it is because we are dead to God. You may not believe in God, but the point remains the same. This is a matter of desire. If you don't desire Jesus, it is because that desire does not exist inside of you. That's just logical. We don't see Christ as beautiful, we don't hear his words as satisfying, and we don't long for his dwelling in our souls, so it makes total sense to say that we are not alive inside to him.

This is the startling biblical picture of sinners apart from God. We are not merely religiously disabled persons needing assistance. We are not drowning in the water, waving our arms and shouting for help. The biblical picture is that, spiritually speaking, we are corpses bobbing in the water. We don't need a life preserver; we need life.

Next, Paul claims that we follow the prince of the power of the air, which is a reference to Satan. He does not mean that people who don't follow Jesus are in the occult or into witchcraft or Satanism. He is taking us right back to the beginning of sin's hostile takeover of the world. Adam and Eve were created in God's image and given the noble mission of spreading God-centered culture throughout their sphere of influence. Then Satan came along and began to whisper sweet lies into their ears.

The serpent in Genesis 3 tempts Eve, and by extension Adam, with taking of the fruit of the tree of the knowledge of good and evil. This was the one tree God commanded them not to eat. The serpent suggests to the first couple, however, that God is holding out on them. He suggests that if they eat that forbidden fruit, they will experience a satisfaction they could not find in God, a wisdom they could not find in God, and a beauty they could not find in God.

People who reject God today, whether actively or passively, are making the same choice. They are deciding that some other thing or some other person will satisfy, enlighten, and enthrall more than God will. According to the Christian worldview, this is buying into the lie of the serpent, asserting our own self-centeredness, our own godhood if you will, and rebelling against God's rightful place as God. This is why Paul says that sinners apart from Christ are devil-followers.

Maybe you don't buy that, but you'd have a difficult time denying the third harsh claim about humanity. Paul says we are appetite-driven—specifically, that we live "in the passions of our flesh, carrying out the desires of the body and the mind." Many people acknowledge this and celebrate it! The magazine covers at the grocery store checkout line seem to revel more and more in the desires of the body and mind, and who could deny that our culture is swimming in the daily allure of the "passions of the flesh"?

The picture that Paul is casting here, however, is not of sexual freedom or libidinous joy but rather slavery. We are like animals, rooting around in the garbage for some satisfying morsel. We are like dogs in heat, unable to restrain our lusts. We are captive to our appetites. I think this explains why those drug addicts in Rutland can't just snap their fingers and suddenly not desire to do drugs anymore. And I think it explains why when I'm having a very rough day, I suddenly find the idea of a big fat milkshake very appealing. These allures have different ramifications, but they are both appetite-driven pursuits of satisfaction.

Finally, Paul stops describing us and decides to categorize us. Apart from life in Christ, we are dead, devil-following, appetite-driven *children of wrath*. Because God is infinitely holy and perfectly righteous, when we fall short of his glory through our rebellious disobedience we become deserving of condemnation.

By following our pride and its lusts, we have turned inward, grotesquely distorting the image of God with which we've been imprinted. We are sacred mirrors, yes, but these mirrors are broken. Where we once perfectly reflected the glory of God conveyed to us by his radiant favor, now we are dim, cracked, turned downward. And by choosing to deny God's glory, we choose his judgment.

But this is not the end of the story. Christianity is not fundamentally a bad news religion. We have to have that bad news, mind you. We have to have it, because it is finally someone shooting straight with us. We can trust God to be honest with us about our true state. But let's be totally honest ourselves: you can find bad news almost anywhere. Good news, on the other hand, is incredibly hard to come by. So what an amazing thing that Paul would describe humanity as desperately wicked and depressingly hopeless, only to unveil this great reversal found in the very next verses: "But God, being rich in mercy, because of the great love with which he loved us, even when we were dead in our trespasses, made us alive together with Christ—by grace you have been saved" (vv. 4–5).

Ephesians 2 is so stunning. The situation could not be worse for us. We are dead. We are devil-worshipers. We are appetite-driven animals. We are children of wrath.

BUT GOD!

BUT GOD!

BUT GOD!

The door has opened. Light is streaming in! It was hopeless and helpless. We were lost and alone and in the dark and hanging over the fires of hell. Nothing we could do could save us from the eternal damnation of the wrath we so deserved and *still* deserve.

BUT GOD!

James Montgomery Boice said, "If you understand those two words—'but God'—they will save your soul."[2]

Two sweet words start the reversal of destiny. Two words that part the sea and roll back the darkness. Two little words like wings of a seraph, breaking through our tomb with a bright ray of light and lifting us up and through the spiritual aether, seating us in the "heavenly places" of Ephesians 2:6.

The great big God of heaven and earth is not only just and righteous and holy but also the merciful justifier of

2. As quoted in Casey Lute, *But God: The Two Words at the Heart of the Gospel* (Hudson, OH: Cruciform Press, 2010), 5.

those who will trust in him. We were going to hell, because God is perfect in holiness, but we are going to heaven, because God is rich in mercy!

We are much worse than we think. But we are more loved than we know.

This is the kind of tension you will only find in Christianity. It is the reason that Christians tuned in to the freedom found in Christ are so often remarkably confident while at the same time remarkably humble. They feel in their bones that they are both deeply broken people and deeply loved people. This kind of thinking must have a profound effect on us.

So Christians oughtn't run around like joyless nitwits, sucking up everybody's fun and wielding the law of God like some kind of rhetorical hammer. We're too sinful ourselves for that.

But Christians also oughtn't run around like licentious hedonists, affirming everyone's dysfunction and cheapening grace like it isn't grounds for repentance. We're too captivated by God's love for that.

The Face of Evil and of Love

What does an evil person look like?

In the wake of the 2013 Boston Marathon bombings, a not-unexpected thing happened in the social media sleuthing for the perpetrators. As readers of popular sites like Reddit pored over photos of the marathon public, they began to highlight suspicious looking figures. And by "suspicious," many meant bag-lugging figures of potentially

Middle Eastern countenance or some other vague non-white descriptor. Some, of course, in both the mainstream and the alternative media insisted (hoped?) the bomber(s) would be white, homegrown terrorists. But in both cases everyone sort of assumed they knew what evil looked like in this instance.

Then something strange happened. The photos of the bombers were released by the FBI. Turns out the perpetrators looked a little like everybody's diverging presumptions assumed they would. Tamerlan and Dzhokhar Tsarnaev weren't homegrown, perhaps, but they were sort of home-raised. They were Muslims, yes, but not Middle Eastern. From Russia's Caucasus region, these fellows were literally from the place from which we get the word *Caucasian*.

Tamerlan was a little easier for our know-it-all eyes to read. The older brother with more visibly evident militant leanings—YouTube clips, hearsay from attenders at the local mosque and even family, concerns from Moscow about terror links, a much-reported trip to Russia the previous year.

But Dzhokhar? As my wife said, "He looks like just a baby." Lots of people were echoing that sentiment. The very face of Dzhokhar—young, somewhat doe-eyed, moppy-haired like every other teenage boy in my town and probably yours—demanded the label "patsy."

From the minute the two were identified, speculators saw only his face and his place in the birth order and deduced he was coerced by his older brother, probably against his will, or duped somehow. Some suggested he was set up by the government.

When the media began to interview Dzhokhar's former teachers and current classmates and friends, the insistence became deafening: "He is not the type of person who would do this," "He's laid back," we were told. "He's cool. He listens to rap music and drinks beer (plays beer pong, even!) and smokes pot and gets with girls, which means he is not a radical Muslim. Which means he's not evil!" Or so they'd say.

What exactly does evil look like, again?

Certainly not like the typical college kid, right? But then I think we need only see what this college kid did in the immediate days after he set down a backpack near children in order to murder them. He went to the gym to work out. He went to a party. (Friends say nothing seemed out of the ordinary.) He tweeted.

I am inclined to think that even if you were coerced, duped, and pressured to murder three innocent people (and a fourth a few days later) and injure many others, you would not act so nonchalant afterward. Nonchalance about one's evil actions is *exactly* the face of evil.

And the idea that someone like a "chill" college kid could never murder anybody is simply ignorance. We know this from countless other newspaper headlines but we also just know it inside. Just a few years of doing pastoral counseling has reaffirmed for me that "normal" people can do some very terrible things. Just a few moments of heart introspection will affirm that I am—and you are—quite apt at murderous thoughts, at the very least.

So what does evil look like?

I think it looks like you and me.

But then there's this: nobody is beyond hope. Nobody is beyond redemption. There is no sin so great that God's gospel is not greater still. Make no mistake: God is holy and just. It is not graceless to suggest that Dzhokhar's older brother has already begun his eternal damnation. But it is graceless to suggest that it is the only option awaiting Dzhokhar himself. The same apostle Paul who served and died for Christianity was previously one of its leading opponents and most violent persecutors. When he talks about the difference between being dead apart from Jesus and being alive in Jesus, he knows what he's talking about.

And as long as Dzhokhar Tsarnaev is breathing, there is time to repent and believe. For he who knew no sin became sin for us, that we might be called the righteousness of God (2 Cor. 5:21).

If that offends you, I don't think you know what the face of evil looks like. Or the face of love.

Something happens, though, when we keep our eyes on Jesus. When we find the courage to take our eyes off ourselves, to stop rooting around in the pigsty of our culture for any piece of filth that smells like it might satisfy and turn our face toward the heavens. We feel the sunlight. The broken mirror of our soul begins to pick up that radiant glow. And what do we see?

In 2 Corinthians 3:18, the same Paul who despaired about feeling caught between good and bad, the same Paul who said that apart from God we are devil-worshiping dogs in heat, says that if we will keep our face turned to Jesus, we will be transformed. In fact, he says that by gazing intently at Jesus's glory, we will be changed, more and more, to resemble Jesus.

See, Jesus is the image of the invisible God. He is the picture of perfect humanity. There is no sin in him. There is no deficiency in his soul. He is not disordered, sexually or otherwise. He is not like us.

But during his time on earth he was like us. He was human. You could hurt him. He slept and wept and bled. He ate and drank and laughed. He loved and he hated. And he was tempted like all of us.

And he didn't pull the divine parachute. Philippians 2:6 says he did not take advantage of any loophole available to him on account of his deity. Despite being fully God, he committed to the experience of being fully man. And this meant dying.

So the perfect mirror of God consented to becoming broken. And he did this so that anybody who would stop going their own way and look to him might see their brokenness restored.

The goal of humanity then, as fantastic and as frail as we are, is not simply to become fully functional human beings but to become like Jesus. And it's a rather remarkable and glorious thing that, as we become more like Jesus, we become more like our unique true selves.

5

Not Just a Good Teacher

HOW JESUS CLAIMED TO BE GOD

The small trailer smelled of rotting food and urine. It was difficult to find a place to sit, but I moved some damp newspapers from a tattered seat and sat down next to the woman who had called me to visit her. Her voice was urgent and her tone was insistent. She needed to see me *right now*.

This was when I was still pastoring in a small, rural town, and I had grown somewhat accustomed to being summoned to the homes of strangers in moments of crisis. It sort of comes with the gig of small-town pastor to be regarded, in some respects, as a chaplain for the wider community. But this woman had given me no real indication on the phone of her needs beyond that she was worried about her son-in-law.

It turned out that her son-in-law was near death, but I found it very odd that she barely wanted to talk about him. Instead, after I'd arrived at her little mobile home filled with all kinds of clutter—full grocery bags, stacks of magazines, dirty dishes piled everywhere—she just wanted to talk to me about her life and about Jesus.

The woman was a disheveled mess herself, a seventy-something vision of disarray in a dingy housecoat and slippers. She talked my ear off about her life as a secretary in New York for a high-rolling financial lawyer, about all the real estate she used to own but had to sell, about her teenage years modeling. She reminisced dramatically, making grand sweeping gestures with her arms and speaking with great theatrical flourish. It did not surprise me to hear her say she used to be an actress, as well.

But now she was here in this little trailer in Vermont, desperate, I assumed, for someone to listen to her.

As someone who feels a real connection to the spiritual world, I sensed a great deal of oppression in the place. Not just from the abundant and malodorous evidence of her life as a hoarder, but from the spiritual relics I noticed around her living room and kitchen. Native American dream catchers hung on the wall and little idols of gods like Ganesh and the Buddha lined the shelves. And all around the walls hung a series of images of Jesus. Only Jesus looked *different*. In almost every picture, Jesus featured a bindi on his forehead, one of the painted "dots" common among Indian and Asian cultures.

My host noticed my curiosity and began to tell me about this Jesus on her walls.

"I know you've read the Bible," she said, "because you're a pastor, but that doesn't mean you know everything."

"Of course not," I said.

"I bet you don't know what Jesus was doing during his middle years."

"You mean between childhood and adulthood?"

"Right," she said. "The Bible shows him being born, then once as a child, and then he's an adult. What happened in those missing years?"

"He was growing up, I suppose," I said. "Probably learning his father's trade."

"Wrong," she said, and quite loudly. "He was in an ashram in India, studying from the maharishi."

I don't remember what I said in response to this. It is likely that I just stared at her blankly. I might have said, "Really?" but not out of curiosity, more out of bemusement.

She went on for a very long time after, and as I felt more and more theologically assaulted, I also felt more and more spiritually oppressed. She talked about Jesus's "third eye," about his learning how to do miracles from Indian shamans, about the purification rituals he would have undergone, and the more detailed she got, the more frenzied she became. At some point she wanted to read my palm.

I know lots of messy Christians, so I'm sure not trying to draw an automatic correlation here, but I believe there was a not-incidental connection between her wild beliefs about Jesus and the disorder and dysfunction so obvious in her home. This woman was quite likely a disturbed individual, but in the brief window in which I had a chance to get a word in edgewise, I suggested that in fact Jesus was not an Asian mystic but a Jew from first-century Palestine who probably spent his middle years doing what most young men of his day did during those years—working hard and keeping his head down.

This seemed boring to her. The real story was not dramatic enough. It did not seem exciting enough. So she had adopted her own personal Jesus. And whenever we do this, no matter how we do it, we always get the Jesus we deserve, which is one as dysfunctional as we are and just as powerless to save.

This woman had co-opted bits and pieces from a variety of world religions, applied what resonated most with her to an idol she called "Jesus," and sought to make the Son of God just another spiritual guru. There is nothing more spiritually dangerous, however, than a "safe Jesus."

But this is the kind of Jesus all of us want, deep down inside. We all want the Jesus who just sort of affirms our okay-ness, who turns a blind eye to our disobedience, who doesn't really challenge us to do things we don't already want to do. We want the Jesus who likes all the same people and things we do and dislikes all the same people and things we do. We want the Jesus who promises us all kinds of goodies while making no demands.

We want the Jesus who "knows his place."

The Jesus of the New Testament, however, eats our safe little Jesuses for breakfast. The real Jesus knows his place—at the center of the universe.

And when we actually read what Jesus said and did in the Bible, we find him saying and doing all sorts of things that defy popular, sentimental projections of Jesus as the all-approving sage, the moralistic *koan*-dispenser, the hippie philosopher. We do not find Jesus "the good teacher" in the New Testament. We find someone altogether quite different.

A Kind of Annoying Teacher

Now, Jesus is a very good teacher. There has never been a better teacher than Jesus. He is the smartest man who ever lived, and not just in an intellectual way but in a street-smart and people-smart way. Nobody ever had access to all the facts and feelings of history and human existence like Jesus Christ. This is how he constantly confounded the religious leaders by running theological circles around them. They said he preached as "one with authority," which meant more than simply being a good preacher. It meant they recognized he preached as one who had great mastery of the Scriptures. He seemed to know them as well as their divine Author! Even his religious enemies admitted this.

Jesus knew when to speak and when to be quiet. He knew who to speak harshly to and who to be gentle with. He knew how to answer direct questions and how to respond to questions with more questions. He knew when to stand his ground and when to retreat. He knew when to work miracles and when to deny them. He could cast out demons and make the devil flee, and he could let Roman soldiers torture and execute him.

Jesus, then and now, is not like any other "good teacher" the way most people think of him as a good teacher. But he is the best teacher who ever lived, for lots of reasons, among them the fact that he constantly subverts what a good teacher does. In fact, if we're honest with ourselves and clearly facing the things Jesus taught, we will admit that he could be a pretty annoying teacher!

Just as one example, think of the parables Jesus often told as part of his traveling ministry. Lots of people today consider these homespun stories as "sermon illustrations" of sorts, down-to-earth tales meant to better explain his theological point of view. But they don't seem to land in the way that illustrations are supposed to land, because the disciples often find them confusing and need to have them interpreted. I will confess that I am not the best teacher in the world, but I think if you're having to constantly explain your sermon illustrations because they always leave people scratching their heads, maybe they aren't exactly working!

Then Jesus goes ahead and says something along the lines of, "I speak in parables so they won't understand me" (Luke 8:10).

Well, that's just weird. And kind of annoying.

Who uses illustrations so people won't understand?

Well, Jesus, that's who. So we have to conclude that either Jesus was not a good teacher or that maybe there's a purpose to the parables we don't understand.

Other times, Jesus answers questions with questions and completely discombobulates his questioners. Like this time, for example:

And they came again to Jerusalem. And as he was walking in the temple, the chief priests and the scribes and the elders came to him, and they said to him, "By what authority are you doing these things, or who gave you this authority to do them?" Jesus said to them, "I will ask you one question; answer me, and I will tell you by what authority I do these things. Was the baptism of John from heaven or from man? Answer me." And they discussed it with one another, saying, "If we say, 'From heaven,' he will say, 'Why then did you not believe him?' But shall we say, 'From man'?"—they were afraid of the people, for they all held that John really was a prophet. So they answered Jesus, "We do not know." And Jesus said to them, "Neither will I tell you by what authority I do these things." (Mark 11:27–33)

I'm sorry, but this is just really cool. This is some Jason Bourne-meets-the-Matrix level of rhetorical jujitsu. Jesus, as the kids say, just schooled these jokers.

But what is Jesus doing? Is he just playing around? Is he trying to embarrass the religious leaders for sport? No, I don't think so. He's not just dodging their questions either. I think by responding to their specific questions with specific questions of his own, Jesus is proving that he is in fact a very good teacher by taking his interlocutors back to their working assumptions. He is exposing their hearts, basically saying, "If you will be honest with me about your convictions concerning me, I will deal with you straightforwardly. But if you come at me with cunning, I will always frustrate you." That's a good teacher, even if an annoying one.

Another time, Jesus himself drills down into the heart of what it even means to think of him as a good teacher:

And as he was setting out on his journey, a man ran up and knelt before him and asked him, "Good Teacher, what must I do to inherit eternal life?" And Jesus said to him, "Why do you call me good? No one is good except God alone."(10:17–18)

This guy just thought he was paying Jesus a compliment. But Jesus won't hear of it. He wants to lay bare what he knows is in the rich man's heart. "You called me 'good.' Think about that. Why would you call me that? Only God is good."

Is Jesus saying that he isn't good? No. But words mean things, and he wants this young man to think through what he was saying. Because if Jesus is teaching that only God is truly good, and if you're going to call Jesus a good teacher, maybe you ought to consider the possibility that Jesus is in fact . . . *nah*. Couldn't be. Could he?

I think Jesus is subtly saying here what he says more directly elsewhere. "I am not just a 'good teacher.' I am God."

And he wants us to think about this. He won't simply let us have him on our own familiar terms, according to our own comfortable terminology. He's pretty annoying that way. But he's also really, really good.

I urge you to consider this. These are things Jesus actually said. You can't simply take him as a good teacher, because where would you get the information to make such a judgment, anyway? From the New Testament, of course. But in the same New Testament people find their "good teacher" Jesus, we see Jesus saying all sorts of difficult, confounding, provocative, and downright offensive things. You can accept those things or reject them, but you can't with any integrity package them up in some safe religious category. My friend in the mobile home tried to do that, and in the end, it was the most unsafe move of all.

A Very Demanding Teacher

Another popular notion people have about Jesus is that he came to make everybody play nice and get along and coexist in a world of behavioral politeness and religious tolerance. Many people, including many Christians, believe that in the Old Testament we had all kinds of codes and restrictions, but then when Jesus came he loosened everything up.

There is a whiff of truth to this, but it is wrong enough to be spiritually dangerous, because once again, it is indicative of trying to mold Jesus according to our preferences and desires.

The truth is that when it came to commandments, Jesus actually makes things harder. Don't believe me? Take a look for yourself:

> For truly, I say to you, until heaven and earth pass away, not an iota, not a dot, will pass from the Law until all is accomplished. Therefore whoever relaxes one of the least of these commandments and teaches others to do the same will be called least in the kingdom of heaven, but whoever does them and teaches them will be called great in the kingdom of heaven. For I tell you, unless your righteousness exceeds that of the scribes and Pharisees, you will never enter the kingdom of heaven. (Matt. 5:18–20)

Basically, Jesus is here saying in his Sermon on the Mount—which many non-Christians look to as the chief evidence that Jesus was all about peace, love, and good vibes—that anyone who slacks off on the Old Testament law is in serious trouble. He's in fact saying that unless someone is perfect, they can't get to heaven. To prove his point, he takes some of those old laws and actually tightens them up!

> You have heard that it was said to those of old, "You shall not murder; and whoever murders will be liable to judgment." But I say to you that everyone who is angry with his brother will be liable to judgment; whoever insults his brother will be liable to the council; and whoever says, "You fool!" will be liable to the hell of fire . . .
>
> You have heard that it was said, "You shall not commit adultery." But I say to you that everyone who looks at a woman with lustful intent has already committed adultery with her in his heart. If your right eye causes you to sin, tear it out and throw it away. For it is better that you lose one of your members than that your whole body be thrown into hell . . .
>
> It was also said, "Whoever divorces his wife, let him give her a certificate of divorce." But I say to you that everyone who divorces his wife, except on the ground of sexual immorality, makes her commit adultery, and whoever marries a divorced woman commits adultery. (vv. 21–22, 27–29, 31–32)

Do you understand what this good teacher has gone and done? He has made things infinitely more difficult. Where the old law told us not to murder, Jesus says not to be angry or insulting. Where the old law told us not to commit adultery, Jesus forbids lust. Where the old law allowed divorce for almost any reason, Jesus reduces the restriction to sexual immorality. This does not sound like a teacher who's making things easier.

I mean, I don't know about you, but I have found it a lot easier not to kill people than not be angry with them. I have never committed physical adultery in my life, but Jesus is saying that if I've lusted after a woman in my heart, I'm just as guilty as anyone who has.

Jesus is in fact a very demanding teacher. He will not let us off the spiritual hook.

When those who do not agree with the Christian view of things ponder these kinds of statements honestly, they must make a decision to trust in Jesus as their only source of salvation or decidedly reject him in his entirety. And here is why those are the only honest responses: Jesus himself does not leave us any other option.

The man never claims to be a religious guru or a "good teacher." He makes outrageous, audacious, scandalous claims about humanity, about God, and about himself. He says things like, "If you don't eat my flesh and drink my blood, you will die," and "I am the way, the truth, and the life; nobody comes to God except through me." He even says things like, "I am the resurrection and the life; if anyone believes in me, he will never die."

"Good teachers" don't say such things. But a *God* teacher would.

Jesus, throughout the New Testament, is in fact placing himself at the center of human existence. This is far above and beyond any other religious leader found in the major world traditions. You may hear some of the things Jesus says about himself on the lips of some leaders of modern-day cults and religious sects. And most of us would consider those people charlatans, hucksters. Very few feel that way about Jesus. We think he is misguided, perhaps. Naive, maybe. But not a liar.

And yet, we can't read what Jesus actually says and think him naive or misguided. He is, as C. S. Lewis famously said, either a liar, a lunatic, or exactly who he says he is.

See, Christianity did not explode in growth in the first centuries because people had found in Jesus a new set of religious instructions. They had found, actually, that the perfection Jesus demanded *he also supplied* to those who trusted in him. They had found that the life Jesus promised he actually delivered!

And people are still discovering this power to be true today. When you modify Jesus and cast him as some kind of safe religious consumer product, you lose the power his words and works actually have, basically because you've lost Jesus.

The Polarizing Teacher

Jesus is magnetic. And repulsive. And this dichotomy would not be true if he was what most moderns want him and assume him to be—a good moral teacher. But Jesus is actually a disruption of the space-time continuum.

Consider this passage from John's Gospel, giving us the fuller context of a verse we examined in chapter 1:

> At that time the Feast of Dedication took place at Jerusalem. It was winter, and Jesus was walking in the temple,

in the colonnade of Solomon. So the Jews gathered around him and said to him, "How long will you keep us in suspense? If you are the Christ, tell us plainly." Jesus answered them, "I told you, and you do not believe. The works that I do in my Father's name bear witness about me, but you do not believe because you are not among my sheep. My sheep hear my voice, and I know them, and they follow me. I give them eternal life, and they will never perish, and no one will snatch them out of my hand. My Father, who has given them to me, is greater than all, and no one is able to snatch them out of the Father's hand. I and the Father are one." (John 10:22–30)

Jesus is saying a plethora of provocative things in this passage, not the least of which is that he and the Father "are one," by which he does not simply mean "in agreement," but actually "on the same level" or, to use more theological parlance, "of the same essence." But he also applies this claim in a provocative way, telling his interrogators that to disbelieve in him is to rule themselves out of the salvation he brings. This flies in the face of universalism and inclusivism, both past and present.

Jesus Christ will never be someone's add-on. He will only be the end-all, be-all.

And while this kind of provocative self-centeredness drives plenty of self-centered people away, it draws a great many to the biblical God.

Time magazine's Mary Eberstadt writes:

Though exact numbers may not always be available, the larger trend is clear: the numerical division between traditionalists and reformers is also seen around the world. It's the stricter Christian churches that typically have stronger and more vibrant congregations—as has been documented at least since Dean M. Kelley's 1996 book, *Why Conservative Churches Are Growing*.

So, for example, the reform-minded Church of England has closed over 1,000 churches since 1980, with some later becoming discos, spas and mosques. The traditionalist Anglican churches of the Global South, on the other hand, are packed to overflowing and still growing fast. Within the Catholic Church, similarly, the most vibrant renewal movements are also the most orthodox. Meanwhile, African missionaries from both Protestant and Catholic churches are being dispatched to the West in record numbers—in effect, re-evangelizing the very peoples who carried the cross to men and women of the subcontinent in the first place . . .

As changing views on gay marriage, among others, go to show, secularization marches on. Traditionalists may be on the losing end of historic real estate, at least for now, as well as booed out of the public square for their views on sex. Down the road, though, they still look to possess something else critical—a growing congregation without which every church, after all, is just a bed and breakfast waiting to happen.[1]

Eberstadt has written a book on this subject called *How the West Really Lost God*, and in it she attributes the growth of what she calls "stricter churches" to a few things, most notably that those passionate about their faith tend to be

1. Mary Eberstadt, "In Battle Over Christianity, Orthodoxy Is Winning," *Time* (April 29, 2013), http://ideas.time.com/2013/04/29/viewpoint-in-the -war-over-christianity-orthodoxy-is-winning/.

more passionate about spreading it, which is true of any religion (including new atheism), but also that conservative religionists tend to be more driven to have children. So, theoretically, we're just outnumbering the irreligious.

But I think when you boil down what is actually happening in harder mission fields—what is taking place in China and portions of Africa, and closer to home what has taken place to move the Pacific Northwest out of its position as the least-churched region of the United States—is that there is something about the exclusivity in conservative, orthodox Christianity that is magnetic.

Why is the exclusivity of Jesus's message compelling? I think we have some clues in that passage in John 10.

The first reason is simply this: you have to respond to Jesus's truth claims. No one can truly be ambivalent about a person's claim to be the center of life, to be God himself. So when Jesus says, "I and the Father are one," the very next thing you see is that they take up stones to kill him.

This is something that keeps happening to Jesus in the Gospels. He preaches in the synagogue near the beginning of his ministry, and for a while they're loving it, but then he ascribes their sacred prophecy of Isaiah to himself, saying in essence that everything in the Hebrew Scriptures is about him, and they want to push him off a cliff.

When you draw a line in the sand, you're going to get a reaction and not always a positive one. Some people are going to reject this message, often with hostility. But others will lean in.

The thing people *can't* do with an exclusive Christianity is truly be apathetic about it. Jesus is clearly forcing the issue now.

I actually think this may be what is contributing to the quiet revival taking place in New England,[2] which at the moment is now the least churched region of the nation[3] and is chock-full of people who claim to love inclusion and tolerance.

Since 1970, the population of Boston has declined but the number of churches in the city has almost doubled, and the number of people attending church has more than tripled in that same period. Across New England, Southern Baptist churches have seen a 20 percent increase over the last decade. The Assemblies of God have increased about the same rate.

Meanwhile, however, the United Churches of Christ, the United Methodist Church, and the Episcopal Church continue to decline. The Anglican Church, on the other hand, is seeing growth.

Now, what do the UCC, the UMC, and the Episcopalians in New England have in common? The answer is this: a "progressive" theology and an inclusive faith that downplays the hard edges of orthodoxy and seeks to adapt Christianity to the prevailing winds of culture.

2. Ruth Graham, "Re-evangelizing New England," *Slate* (November 27, 2012), http://www.slate.com/articles/life/faithbased/2012/11/re_evangelizing_new_england_how_church_planting_and_music_festivals_are.html. See also Rob Moll, "Boston's Quiet Revival," *Christianity Today* (January 25, 2006), http://www.christianitytoday.com/ct/2006/januaryweb-only/104-32.0.html.

3. See Frank Newport, "Church Attendance Lowest in New England, Highest in South," *Gallup* (April 27, 2006), http://www.gallup.com/poll/22579/church-attendance-lowest-new-england-highest-south.aspx.

What do the SBC, the Assemblies of God, and the Anglicans in New England have in common? Well, these different expressions all share an evangelical theology that affirms the authority of Scripture, the forgiveness of sins and escape from hell found exclusively in Christ, and a biblical stance on cultural issues of our day such as abortion and same-sex marriage.

The daughter of the Anglican bishop of New England was a member of my church in Vermont, so I got to spend a little bit of time hearing this bishop's vision for an Anglican church-planting movement in New England. I was blown away. Who knew Anglicans planted churches? Joining them in the Northeast are impressive efforts by the North American Mission Board of the Southern Baptist Convention and some independent churches in the Acts29 Network and in the Association of Related Churches, planting new church after new church to proclaim the gospel of the exclusive Jesus more and more in the least churched region in the nation. And the result? While liberal churches continue to decline in New England, evangelical churches are increasing and filling. There is a slow reformation brewing.

Why? How are evangelical churches with conservative theology preaching this old, old story bringing people to the faith in the hard soil of the Northeast? Well, it seems counterintuitive, but when you draw a line in the sand, you tend to move people.

The progressive logic appears to be that the more all-inclusive we make Jesus, the more appealing he will be to a lost world. The Jesus who judges the quick and the dead in such a way as to consign those who reject him to eternal damnation, the Jesus who demands utter allegiance to himself alone, it is suggested, is too narrow, too exclusive to commend Christianity to those outside the fold. Let's make the circle bigger, we're told, bigger even than explicit belief, because the Jesus who loves and does not hate and plans to bring all individuals into heaven is a more compelling Jesus than the Jesus of the "traditional church."

But history shows us the opposite is the case. Ask the mainline denominations right now if "love wins" in this way. This "bigger" Jesus ironically makes for a smaller following. And this, I think, is why: a Jesus who is all-inclusive and demands no all-forsaking allegiance to himself for salvation and threatens no damnation does not commend others to him; he commends others to sit tight wherever they're at. He would not win people to himself; he would tell them such a thing is unnecessary. Someone who believes that Jesus will save them even if they never believe has no compulsion to believe. They receive assurance without faith.

The universalist Jesus cannot be found in the Gospels; the Jesus we find there is too busy putting himself at the center of everything. The universalist Jesus is safe and safely ignored. It is the compelling Jesus of the Scriptures who refuses to be disregarded.

But there's something else here too. It is something we saw beneath the "arguments surrendered" in the stories of Nancy Pearcey and Francis Collins. It is not simply that Jesus positions himself so that we are either for him or against him. It is that those who find themselves with

Jesus find Jesus with *them*. They find that Jesus answers deep questions not only of intellect and philosophy but of spirit and soul and emotion and wonder. Jesus unlocks the hardened heart and provides the satisfaction, the salvation, and the security that every sinful and broken human being has always wanted.

Only the exclusive Jesus could provide this kind of security.

Now, religious certainty always promises security. Most every religious person across every tradition believes they have finally found the answers to all their questions. But Christianity doesn't simply offer certainty of human will or human intellect. It offers certainty of *divine* will and messianic atonement.

The security Christianity's exclusive gospel offers is different than the security offered by other religions, which all essentially say, "If you can jump through these hoops, you can be saved." That sounds secure but there are too many variables involved.

Christianity says, "No hoops. Only Jesus."

Christianity offers the kind of security, in fact, that says, "There's nothing you could do to make God love you less."

This simply flies in the face of most people's perceptions of God. Like the Muslim cab driver I told you about in chapter 1, most people believe that—if there is a God—there are some things he couldn't forgive and still claim to be holy.

But we don't have a God who turns a blind eye to murder. He punishes every murder; he punishes every sin. It's just that, for those who repent of their sins and believe in Jesus Christ, the punishment is given to Christ on the cross.

This kind of exclusivity—grace is exclusive to Christianity and grace is exclusive to those who trust in Christ— provides the best kind of security because it posits that refuge from God's wrath is only found in God himself.

Jesus says in John 10:28, "I give them eternal life, and they will never perish, and no one will snatch them out of my hand."

There is no greater security than this! To be found in Christ's immovable, unconquerable hand. What a gift!

And if I am in Christ's hand, I am united to Christ. And if I am united to Christ, never to be snatched away, then really I am as secure as Christ is. The freedom that comes from this reality is extraordinarily compelling. Who doesn't want to know they are eternally secure?

It is in this way—in the way of Jesus Christ, in the Jesus Christ who alone is the Way—that Christianity stands alone.

+ + + + **6** +

Winning by Dying

HOW JESUS TRIUMPHED
OVER EVIL AND INJUSTICE

Despite being a kid, basically, he was still pretty much a "tough guy," a native Vermonter raised in the woods, made strong by hunting and farming and chopping wood. And as he sat in the chair opposite my desk in the pastor's study, practically weeping, I knew it had to have been a hard thing to approach me for help.

He was not a particularly religious guy, but his girl-friend was, and she had broken up with him. Somehow he'd summoned up the courage to approach the religious professional for some relationship advice.

"So what do I do?" he asked.

"Um, well, you know." I tried to sound casual, comforting, consoling. "You just take it a day at a time, I guess."

"No," he said. "I mean, to get her back."

"Oh."

"She's the greatest thing that's ever happened to me."

"Okay."

"I really love her."

"I see that."

"So what do I do?"

I wondered if he was looking for some help with a grand romantic gesture, a way of winning her heart back once and for all. The truth was, I didn't want them to be together. And neither did lots of people, including the girl's parents.

He was a really nice guy. We had nothing against him personally. But he wasn't a Christian. His girlfriend claimed that she was. She had heard enough counsel from those who loved her to understand we didn't think seriously dating somebody who didn't share her convictions about the things of faith was a good idea. Further, I'd suggested that contemplating a relationship that headed toward marriage with someone who wasn't a believer in Jesus could be an indication she didn't take her convictions about faith all that seriously either.

Eventually she broke up with him, although I don't know if it had anything to do, really, with her religious commitments. I think she just sort of outgrew the relationship.

But as far as this young man knew, she had broken up with him because he wasn't a Christian. So now he was in my office wanting to know what he should do about it.

"I should start reading my Bible more, right?"

"Well, sure."

"And praying."

"Well, yeah. Prayer is important."

"I've been coming to church with her every week, but I can keep coming even if we don't sit together."

"Yes, I'd hate to see you stop coming."

"And do you think," he said, "you'd put a word in for me?"

"I'm sorry?" I asked.

"Like, could you talk to her? Tell her I'm really trying? I miss her so much. I've never loved anyone like I love her."

She was his first love. I knew the pain well. I was always the guy suffering from unrequited crushes myself. I was always the guy parents wanted their daughters to date, which is a great way to become the guy nobody's daughters wanted to date. So I felt for him. And I didn't want to further break his heart. But I had to.

"Look," I said, "reading your Bible, praying, and coming to church are all great things, and I hope you will do them. But I have to tell you, if you're only doing these things to get your girlfriend back, it's not going to work. I don't really know how to get her back, and I don't know if you guys should even be together, but I do know that if you're going to try the religious stuff, you have to actually do it because you love Jesus."

He hung his head but kept his heartbroken gaze on my face.

"Because I have to tell you," I said, "that Jesus is better than anybody else. And if you're only using Christianity to get things you want, you won't be Christian for very long and you won't even end up satisfied if you do get what you want. If you're going to do the Christian thing, it has to be because you want Jesus."

The conversation was effectively over at that point. He nodded, wiped his glistening eyes, thanked me for my time, and left. He came to church a few more times, but dropped out soon enough.

I really liked the guy. And I really felt bad for him. But I wanted him to know a love much greater than the love of any woman. That wasn't what he wanted, so he walked away disappointed.

In a way, the situation reminded me of Jesus's encounter with the rich young ruler. This man came looking for some kind of validation of his own righteousness, a spiritual stamp of approval for all his good deeds and good intentions. He wanted approval for all the things he was already willing to do.

And then Jesus exposed his true god. Jesus told him to go sell all of his possessions and give them away to the poor. The man walked away depressed, because he'd been asked to trade in his real object of worship for Jesus.

I'd done the same thing to this young man. His girlfriend had become an idol in his life, to the point where he was willing to go through some religious motions to "worship" her and win the "salvation" of being in a relationship with her. And then here I came, asking him to give her up, and I only crushed his heart further.

This is a dynamic we find occurring over and over again in the Bible. People keep coming to God with their hopes and dreams attached to things he may or may not give them, and many of them leave disappointed when he suggests that, in fact, not getting those things is the best thing for them.

For instance, wealth in the Bible is not considered sinful but it is considered extremely dangerous. Riches are depicted as a blessing from God to be stewarded wisely. Jesus issues lots of warnings about riches. He knows how easy it is for money and things to become our gods.

But, really, anything can become a god to us, including good things. Human beings are exceptional worshipers. None of us is ever not worshiping. Whatever we are deriving our ultimate satisfaction from, whatever is our source of fulfillment and supreme joy, wherever it is we find our fundamental identity and essential worth and meaning—that is our god. Even atheists have gods.

Over and over again, the Bible identifies idolatry as the root sin keeping humanity from God. And over and over again, the Bible calls us to, in effect, kill our idols. We have to be willing to lay our gods on the altar of sacrifice in order to experience the one true God who will give us real life, full of satisfaction and supremely delicious in joy.

The Totally Projected Outcome Nobody Expected

Have you ever seen M. Night Shyamalan's film *Signs*? Starring Mel Gibson and Joaquin Phoenix, it is ostensibly about an alien invasion but it's really a fairly decent meditation on faith. Gibson plays a rural pastor whose wife has died in a car accident, leaving him to care for their two young children and his brother, Merrill. His grief has created a great crack in his relationship with God and he begins to question his faith.

Then the crop circles start showing up. The mystery is sustained for most of the film, and at one point he says to his brother, "See, what you have to ask yourself is what kind of person are you? Are you the kind that sees signs, that sees miracles? Or do you believe that people just get lucky? Or, look at the question this way: Is it possible that there are no coincidences?"

This idea—that there are no coincidences—becomes a thematic banner over the rest of the story, culminating in the convergence of the memory of his wife's dying words ("Tell Merrill to swing away") with the annoying habit of their little girl (leaving half-finished glasses of water all over the house). In the climactic scene when the aliens have finally infiltrated the house, Merrill finds himself, baseball bat in hand, facing off against one of the otherworldly creatures in a room decorated with half-full water glasses. Water, it so happens, is like poison to the aliens, so Merrill "swings away," smashing the glasses and spraying deadly water onto his opponent.

Okay, it's a little silly as a plot point. But if you're tracking with the faith angle, it is sort of clever and impressive. All of these little things, these signs, add up to this one climactic moment. The little girl's frustrating routine of leaving glasses everywhere has a meaning! (My fourteen-year-old also leaves half-finished glasses of water all over the house, and when I complain, she's taken to telling me she's just preparing us for the alien invasion.) All of the glasses were just waiting for their appointed time to make sense.

There is a moment in Luke's Gospel when the resurrected Jesus comes alongside two of his disciples on the road to a place called Emmaus, and we are told that he reveals everything to them about himself as found in the Hebrew Scriptures. Basically, Jesus walks these faithful Jews from Genesis through the prophets, showing them all the glasses of water.

This is such a helpful thing for him to do. And what a glorious walk and talk that must have been!

But we see in the Gospels just how dense Jesus's audience seems to be, even as he's point-by-point fulfilling and satisfying so many of the prophecies and requirements expected to accompany the messiah. I think if this shows us anything, it's how blind we can be to things before our eyes *if we don't want to see them.*

In Jesus's day, the messianic expectation was huge and boisterous. The Jewish people longed for their coming deliverer. Living under Roman occupation and oppression, they tended to assume that God's anointed one would arrive in military fashion, riding a horse and swinging a sword. But then when Jesus carries out his triumphal entry into the city of Jerusalem, he comes riding on a donkey underneath the green wave of palm branches. He did have many worshipers gathered that day, but so many of them abandoned him by the end of the week. Why? It's not like they didn't know the prophecy of Zechariah 9:9:

> Rejoice greatly, O daughter of Zion!
>   Shout aloud, O daughter of Jerusalem!
> Behold, your king is coming to you;
>   righteous and having salvation is he,

> humble and mounted on a donkey,
> on a colt, the foal of a donkey.

By welcoming Jesus into town this way, they were fulfilling this very prophecy, and yet when the time came to side with the one true king, these same revelers departed.

But Jesus's life and ministry is not contingent upon the people around him "getting it." We have the benefit of hindsight now, especially the interpretive hindsight of the New Testament, but it's hard to imagine someone could hear Jesus teach and not see the perfect alignment with the messianic vision of the Hebrew Bible. We see it now. And it is mind-boggling just how many Jewish descriptions of great specificity fit this person we call Jesus of Nazareth.

All along, the life and ministry of Jesus are too good *not* to be true. Over and over again we see how the things he's saying and doing are not improvised but *authored*—authored as if there is a sovereign plan in place. Here is just a short list of examples of Old Testament prophecies and descriptions about the messiah that were fulfilled in the life and ministry of Jesus:

- He would be born of a virgin (Isa. 7).
- He would be born in Bethlehem (Mic. 5:2).
- He would be betrayed by a close friend (Ps. 55).
- He would be rejected by his people (Isa. 53).
- He would have his hands and feet pierced while enemies gambled for his clothes (Isa. 53 and Ps. 22).
- He would be given vinegar to drink (Ps. 69).
- None of his bones would be broken (Ps. 34).

These are just the highlights. There are more.

Now, the skeptic reads things like this and thinks to himself, *Well, of course he fulfilled these prophecies. If he was familiar with them, he'd know to do things in line with them.* But this kind of reasoning misses just how many messianic prophecies fulfilled in the life of Jesus were contingent upon the actions of so many other parties. Here's one rather odd example, found in Zechariah 11:12–13:

> I said to them, "If it is good in your sight, give me my wages; but if not, never mind!" So they weighed out thirty shekels of silver as my wages. Then the LORD said to me, "Throw it to the potter, that magnificent price at which I was valued by them." So I took the thirty shekels of silver and threw them to the potter in the house of the LORD. (NASB)

It just so happened that Jesus was betrayed for thirty pieces of silver, which was then used to buy a place called Potter's Field.

How's your mind? Blown?

Well, wait; there's more. At least sixty-one major messianic prophecies found in the Old Testament were fulfilled by Jesus in the New Testament, including really specific things he could not have willfully controlled, like his place of birth.

Peter Stoner determined the probability of one man fulfilling just eight of the prophecies of the Old Testament for the Messiah to be 1 in 10—to the 17th power (a quadrillion).

> [Suppose that] we take 10^{17} silver dollars and lay them on the face of Texas. They will cover all of the state two

feet deep. Now mark one of these silver dollars, and stir the whole mass thoroughly, all over the state. Blindfold a man and tell him that he can travel as far as he wishes, but he must pick up one silver dollar and say that this is the right one. What chance would he have of getting the right one? Just the same chance that the prophets would have had of writing these eight prophecies and having them all come true in any one man, from their day to the present time, providing they wrote them in their own wisdom.

Now these prophecies were either given by inspiration of God or the prophets just wrote them as they thought they should be. In such a case the prophets had just one chance in 10^{17} of having them come true in any man, but they all came true in Christ.

This means that the fulfillment of these eight prophecies alone proves that God inspired the writing of those prophesies to a definiteness which lacks only one chance in 10^{17} of being absolute.[1]

Stoner then goes on to consider the possibility of any one person fulfilling forty-eight of the prophecies by chance. Here the odds jump to 1 in 10 to the 157th power.

So you tell me? Are you the kind of person who believes in coincidences?

I think there are no coincidences. And even if there were, this is a startling number of them connected to the most central historical figure in world history. There is no such preponderance of prophetic evidence surrounding Mohammed or the Buddha or Krishna.

1. As quoted in Josh McDowell, *A Ready Defense* (Nashville: Thomas Nelson, 1993), 213.

And yet Jesus fulfills so many of these obvious messianic predictions and still gets rejected by his countrymen. What gives?

I think it has a lot to do with the unassuming way he took over the world. Jesus's way of winning looks a lot like losing sometimes. His way of living looks a lot like dying.

Turning Things Right Side Up

Jesus's way of setting things back to rights often looks a lot like stirring stuff up! Into the world of the Roman Empire and Jewish oppression, Christ came preaching "the gospel of the kingdom," declaring that God's kingdom was now actually "at hand" in and through himself, and announcing that anyone could achieve access to this kingdom by denying themselves. To *live*, basically, you had to die to yourself. This is what "taking up your cross" means.

Jesus paints the perfect picture of this kingdom in his life and ministry as he and his disciples actually lived it—with Jesus at the center as true Lord and King—in the midst of a world that lived as though Herod was king and Caesar was lord. In the Gospel of Matthew, Jesus announces the invasion of his kingdom into the world with his version of the Magna Carta, the Declaration of Independence, and the Constitution all rolled into one. We call it the Sermon on the Mount.

The Sermon on the Mount (Matt. 5–7) is a great kingdom blueprint, a beautiful proclamation of what the kingdom of God *looks like*. It begins with the gospel of the beatitudes (which is a preamble, essentially saying, "Look, this is how it's going to be now") and continues to outline a glorious reality that hums and buzzes with life in the Spirit. In nearly every way, the Sermon on the Mount runs counter to the way of the world, and today it calls out to us to abandon self-interest, embrace the dangerous life of discipleship, and live counterculturally.

The temptation for us is to look at the Sermon on the Mount and read it as law rather than good news. We look at it and see it as things to *do*. And it is. But the Sermon on the Mount, as a picture of the kingdom, is also (and best) thought of as something to *be*.

What we see in the Sermon on the Mount is a sweeping survey of how to live in the kingdom, complete with commands ("Turn the other cheek," etc.), but if we read it as law, we miss the stunning truth that the kingdom is something that already exists and which Jesus is bringing. It is the difference between "making" Jesus king and recognizing that he already is. It speaks not just to Christian behavior but first and foremost to Christian character. And this is why Jesus reframes so many things like adultery (to lust) and murder (to anger)—so we won't see Christianity firstly as something to do but something to *be*.

Jesus is instituting nothing less than the fundamental reordering of humanity and the entire social order, all when set in orbit around himself. Consider this teaching from his Sermon on the Mount, from the prelude we call the beatitudes:

> Blessed are the poor in spirit, for theirs is the kingdom of heaven.
> Blessed are those who mourn, for they shall be comforted.

Blessed are the meek, for they shall inherit the earth.
Blessed are those who hunger and thirst for righteousness,
  for they shall be satisfied.
Blessed are the merciful, for they shall receive mercy.
Blessed are the pure in heart, for they shall see God.
Blessed are the peacemakers, for they shall be called sons
  of God.
Blessed are those who are persecuted for righteousness'
  sake, for theirs is the kingdom of heaven.
Blessed are you when others revile you and persecute you
  and utter all kinds of evil against you falsely on my ac-
  count. (Matt. 5:3–11)

While the spirit of our age appeals to our desire to mas-
ter ourselves and others, the kingdom calls for humility,
for self-denial, for decrease. The messiah-king everyone
expected in Jesus's day was a revolutionary hero, a military
warrior who would violently overthrow the kingdoms of
the world in order to establish the kingdom of God. Instead they got a foot-washing carpenter. While the world
was looking for a zealot, instead they got a servant. Jesus
himself declares the success of this reversal in the beatitudes
when he says, "Blessed are the meek, for they shall inherit
the earth" (v. 5).

Soon thereafter, Jesus begins talking about going a second mile with someone who demands the first, giving to
anyone who makes requests, and—scariest of all—loving
our enemies. In all of this what we see is the upside-down
nature of kingdom subversion. The kingdoms of the world
trade in rhythms like accumulation, force, appearance, and
individualism. But the kingdom of God posits rhythms

that rely on God's power, not ours, and that emerge from and point to the greatness of God, not the greatness of ourselves.

The way to enlist in the kingdom is to humble yourself, and the way to war for the kingdom is to give of yourself and serve. "For even the Son of Man did not come to be served," Mark 10:45 tells us, "but to serve, and to give His life a ransom for many" (NASB).

The problem is that in sin we are constantly using others. We practice relational legalism, expecting others to serve us or to contribute to our own well-being. Our feelings or approval become the measure of righteousness and we disdain any who do not meet the mark. We say to others, explicitly or implicitly, that we will serve them after they've earned it somehow. This is what that young man was saying in my office when he was asking for help winning his girlfriend back. He wanted to use Christianity to earn his girlfriend. But using things to get what we want is diametrically opposed in value to Christianity itself.

The beatitudes turn this value system upside down. And in doing so, Jesus plans to turn the world right side up.

The primary way he does this is by his death.

Killing Death from the Inside

No one can say that Jesus did not have the courage of his convictions. And just as the Old Testament continually seeds the idea of Christ Jesus coming, Christ Jesus is continually seeding the idea with his disciples that he has come to die.

His followers seem mostly ignorant, somehow deaf to what he is saying. It's similar to the way most of Jesus's fellow Jews couldn't see his fulfillment of their prophecies. Sometimes his followers get clued in. And when they are, they object to his talk about death. It offends them. It doesn't seem befitting the true king.

But in Jesus's estimation, the only way to actually establish his reign and dominion is to die for the sins of the world and, through that death, actually defeat the earth's ultimate enemy. Jesus is going to stare death in the face and defeat it. It is in this way that Jesus plans to conquer the world.

"And I," Jesus says, "when I am lifted up from the earth"—he means on the cross—"will draw all people to myself" (John 12:32).

And something earth-shatteringly wonderful happens when Jesus dies on the cross. The Bible tells us that the veil in the temple, separating the most holy place, is torn from top to bottom. Through the sacrifice of Christ, God has destroyed the division between himself and sinners. What death ruined, Jesus has fixed. He's putting the place right side up.

This means standing victorious at the pinnacle of creation, and it means defeating definitively the enemies of God. The Bible says that Jesus does all of this *by dying*.

> [He canceled] the record of debt that stood against us with its legal demands. This he set aside, nailing it to the cross. He disarmed the rulers and authorities and put them to open shame, by triumphing over them in him. (Col. 2:14–15)

This is why Christians refer to the day their religious founder died as Good Friday. Because what Jesus accomplished on the cross was exceedingly good! This offends so many religious and irreligious sensibilities. Jews do not think messiahs get victimized. Muslims do not think men can be saviors. Moralists do not think Jesus's death enacted any kind of atonement.

> For the word of the cross is folly to those who are perishing, but to us who are being saved it is the power of God. For it is written, "I will destroy the wisdom of the wise, and the discernment of the discerning I will thwart." (1 Cor. 1:18–19)

In what other religion could you get this? Oh, sure, you can find martyrs for the causes aplenty. But can you find a God-Man who goes willingly to his own death to pay the penalty for sin so that men and women might be forgiven forever and freed from death?

No, you cannot.

And Jesus goes even further than that. By receiving the full brunt of the wrath of God for sin, he rises nailed to the intersection of justice and mercy only to be lowered into the grave, a dead man. And there he turns death itself upside down.

You Can't Keep a God-Man Down

HOW JESUS DEFEATED DEATH

To really solidify my reputation as a pastoral match-*un*-maker, I have to tell you about this engaged couple who came to ask if I would officiate their wedding. Now, I have this personal policy, a conscience thing for me, that prevents me from overseeing the nuptials involving someone who doesn't believe in Jesus Christ as their Lord and Savior. I know lots of ministers are different, and I respect that. But as one who takes covenant vows seriously and would be reading from Scripture and calling grooms to love their wives as Christ loved his bride, the church, and calling brides to trust and respect their husbands like the church does Christ, I would find it difficult to expect someone who doesn't believe in Jesus or the Bible to mean those vows. It would simply be a religious ceremony, and I'm not too big on religious ceremonies.

So because I don't like to see myself as a provider of religious goods and services, I don't perform weddings for non-Christians.

Well, as you can imagine, this doesn't always go over very well. And I remember this one particular couple who just could not seem to understand why I did not want to marry them. I couldn't understand why they would *want* me to! In their mind, employing me and using the church building was a great way to make their wedding look religious without, you know, actually *meaning* the religious stuff. (For some reason, it didn't seem to occur to them that this might be offensive to me, as one who has given my heart and life to this "religious stuff.")

The sticking point came in our premarital interview when I asked the groom-to-be what he believed about Jesus.

"You believe he died?" I asked.

"Oh, sure," he said.

"And that he rose again?"

"Well . . ." He looked over at his fiancée hesitantly. She was more "religious" than he.

"This is pretty important," I said. "What we believe about these things is what actually determines if we're Christians or not."

"Well," he continued, "couldn't we say that he lived again inside his followers?"

"We could say that," I said.

"Like, in spirit or whatever."

"Yes, that's true," I conceded. "But it's also true that he actually resurrected. He was dead and he physically, tangibly came back to life. You don't believe that?"

"Well . . . no."

I thanked them for thinking highly enough of me to ask me to marry them, but I explained as politely as I could that I simply couldn't perform the ceremony. In my mind, what I do as a minister of the gospel is help people align their lives with the truth of Jesus. This nice fellow didn't believe Jesus was alive, so administering his marriage vows would have felt to me like a sham.

His fiancée was more upset than he was. He seemed completely nonplussed by the whole thing. I assumed, then, that he really didn't care who performed their ceremony, where they got married, or what he had to say or do to cooperate. She, on the other hand, felt as if I was impugning their Christian credentials.

And I absolutely was.

In 1 Corinthians 15, the apostle Paul says this about the resurrection of Jesus Christ:

> And if Christ has not been raised, then our preaching is in vain and your faith is in vain. We are even found to be misrepresenting God, because we testified about God that he raised Christ, whom he did not raise if it is true that the dead are not raised . . And if Christ has not been

raised, your faith is futile and you are still in your sins. (vv.14–15, 17)

Essentially, he is saying that if Jesus didn't actually come back from the dead, Christianity is pointless. And so claiming to be Christian while not believing in Christ's resurrection is equally pointless. And nonsensical.

So this is a key tenet of orthodox belief in the Christian religion. You can adhere to some of the morals espoused in Christian teaching, you can have a great affection for the traditions of Christian religion, you can enjoy going to church and reading your Bible, but if you don't believe Jesus Christ died, was buried, and then was resurrected, you're not a Christian.

Obviously this is not a popular claim among religionists who identify as "liberal Christians" or "progressive Christians," because many of them believe Jesus only resurrected in spirit or in idea or in the hearts of his followers left behind. But this isn't what the Bible says happened. The witnesses had a real encounter with the breathing and touchable Jesus three days after he died.

Of course things like this don't happen! This is why the resurrection makes Christianity so compelling. Our founder went through death and came out the other side.

They Thought Their Friend Was Gone Forever; You Won't Believe What Happened Next

There is this theory that Jesus's followers perpetrated a sham of their own. Some people think that the disciples somehow stole Jesus's body and then began spreading this wild story about him coming back to life. Kind of a *Weekend at Bernie's* situation, without a body.

But this theory gives the disciples way too much credit and at the same time not enough.

First of all, the idea that this handful of men would have been able to steal a dead body under imperial guard without anybody noticing or raising a stink after the fact is pretty silly. The disciples were not Ocean's Eleven. They were ordinary guys left scattered and devastated after Jesus died. And even if they had been able to gather themselves together in a strong and smart enough way to pull off this grave robbery, all the Romans would have to do is tell people what happened. But they didn't, because it didn't happen. Believing it did gives the disciples way too much credit.

But it also doesn't give them much credit at all, because it assumes that Jesus's followers would have perpetuated such a great lie. It assumes that they would have, in a concentrated way, colluded together to foist a gigantic deception onto the world, that they'd be men of such low character that this would have seemed an agreeable thing to do. And while the disciples aren't exactly geniuses, they aren't exactly lowlifes either.

No, the reality is that the disciples, after Jesus died, more than likely sat around crying, feeling dejected and discouraged. Remember, they had given their lives and their livelihoods to follow Jesus. They really did think he was the messiah. They really did believe he was going to overthrow the enemy and restore the nation of Israel to her previous glory.

So when Jesus was arrested and crucified, they likely began to have second thoughts. In their day, many would-be messiahs had come and gone. Lots of would-be messiahs ended up at the hands of the Romans, usually nailed to crosses. Jesus was not the first.

When someone claiming to be the anointed one of Israel who had come to set the people free was finally executed, his followers typically agreed this was a sign he wasn't the messiah. After a period of mourning, they usually moved on to the next promising prospect, often a family member of the dearly departed.

Although Jesus had been telling his friends all along that he was planning to die, they never quite understood or believed him, and when it happened they likely rethought everything. But they wouldn't have made up the idea of the resurrection for the precise reason you'd think they wouldn't—because it sounds ridiculous.

People don't come back from the dead. Oh, sure, people who flatline are often revived. But Jesus was officially, legally, and lengthily dead. He was executed by professionals who knew their craft. And after three days in the tomb, the decomposition process would have already begun. They had no defibrillator. There weren't even smelling salts. The man had died. And the disciples were not superstitious people. They knew then what we know now—dead people don't come back to life.

Some of Jesus's female followers, including his mother, went to the tomb after the Sabbath to see if they could dress Jesus properly with burial spices. They found the place empty and the stone door moved. Back at Christian

Headquarters, the disciples were not trying to figure out how to start the Jesus's Miracle-Working Reunion Tour but how to not get crucified themselves. I imagine the room they were meeting in was eerily quiet. A lot of soul-searching going on.

I try to put myself in these men's sandals. How would I have felt if I'd given three years of the prime of my life to this man, had sold out completely to his way of life and teaching, had put all my hopes and dreams of deliverance for my people and the eradication of injustice and oppression onto his shoulders, fully expecting him to bring the revolution our national soul had longed for throughout thousands of years—and then I saw him murdered.

I would have been profoundly grieved to have lost such a friend. But I would also have been profoundly depressed to have had my hopes dashed so conclusively.

And then it would feel very cruel when Peter barges in to say he's seen an angel and Jesus isn't in the tomb anymore. It would have been just like Peter to act like such a cruel-hearted, impetuous fool. Peter's the guy who denied Jesus three times, just like Jesus said he would. And now he wants to act like he's had some great epiphany? That's convenient.

And then these two jokers, Cleopas and his friend, burst through the door to say they'd seen Jesus on the road to Emmaus. And the whole thing just seems so mean, and so bewildering, and so awful, and so confusing, and . . .

Well. I mean. What if it's true?

And then suddenly he's there.

Not there in my heart. Not there in my memories. Not there in the aether, like the "spirit of peace" or some such thing.

No, Jesus is actually *there*. Standing there. In the room. Looking at me.

He's asking about lunch.

And some of you think they made this up.

> Jesus himself stood among them, and said to them, "Peace to you!" But they were startled and frightened and thought they saw a spirit. And he said to them, "Why are you troubled, and why do doubts arise in your hearts? See my hands and my feet, that it is I myself. Touch me, and see. For a spirit does not have flesh and bones as you see that I have." And when he had said this, he showed them his hands and his feet. And while they still disbelieved for joy and were marveling, he said to them, "Have you anything here to eat?" They gave him a piece of broiled fish, and he took it and ate before them.
>
> Then he said to them, "These are my words that I spoke to you while I was still with you, that everything written about me in the Law of Moses and the Prophets and the Psalms must be fulfilled." Then he opened their minds to understand the Scriptures, and said to them, "Thus it is written, that the Christ should suffer and on the third day rise from the dead, and that repentance and forgiveness of sins should be proclaimed in his name to all nations, beginning from Jerusalem. You are witnesses of these things." (Luke 24:36–48)

That's what happened. He was dead. Then they were eating fish with him like old times.

We Have a Leader Who Came Back from the Dead

Many Christians observe Advent and celebrate the Christmas season to commemorate Jesus Christ's birth. This is good, because the doctrine of the incarnation (God becoming man) is extremely important. Christians believe Jesus was fully God and fully man, and we have gone to great pains to protect this doctrine from false teaching and heresy. And we've also gone to great pains for this doctrine, enduring persecution and hardship to maintain it.

But the Easter holiday marks the central event in human history. At Easter, Christians celebrate the reality that Jesus the God-Man was killed and then was resurrected. Easter is our holiday to exult in the reality that Jesus has conquered death. Who wouldn't want to celebrate that?

This is why I find it odd every year to see so many Christian churches making a huge deal at Easter time about everything *but* the resurrection. Many churches give away door prizes, gifts of cash, and electronic consumer goods. Some megachurches even give away cars! They know that Easter has great potential for church visitation, so any extra incentive they can think of to get people in the door seems worth it. But all I can ever think about this "cash and prizes" religious bait game is how unamazing it makes the resurrection seem.

I mean, our leader *came back from the dead*. If that doesn't pack 'em in, maybe it's because we don't act like it's all that big of a deal to us. But the Easter event is the biggest deal in the history of big deals.

Easter changes everything. As Jaroslav Pelikan said, "If Christ is risen, nothing else matters. And if Christ is not risen, nothing else matters."[1]

There is no other religion or spiritual movement who can make this claim as credibly as Christianity can make it. We've been toeing this line for two thousand years without fail. We are the only ones bold enough to claim (and believe) that the founder of our religion is actually, physically still alive. In this regard, among many others, Jesus Christ is unparalleled as a historical figure. He stands alone. Bob your head to these Shai Linne lines:

> *Plato is dead, Socrates is dead*
> Aristotle and Immanuel Kant are dead
> Nietzsche and Darwin are dead—however
> Jesus is Alive . . .
>
> Buddha is dead, Mohammed is dead
> Gandhi and Haile Selassie are dead
> Elijah Mohammed is dead—however
> Jesus is Alive . . .
>
> Nero is dead, Constantine is dead
> Genghis Khan and Attila the Hun are dead
> Alexander the Great is dead—however
> Jesus is Alive
>
> Napoleon is dead, Lao Tzu is dead
> Che Guevara and Henry VIII are dead
> Saddam Hussein is dead—however
> Jesus is Alive . . .

1. Jaroslav Pelikan, "In Memoriam," *Yale Department of History Newsletter* (Spring 2007), http://www.learningace.com/doc/2851196/4f2988fe924110ed 3ce00f5f1315b7bd/historynewsletter07f.

Caesar is dead, Herod is dead
Annas, Caiaphas and Judas are dead
Pontius Pilate is dead—however
Jesus is Alive[2]

Muslims don't believe this. Jews don't believe this. Even Jehovah's Witnesses don't believe this. (They say Jesus rose as a kind of "spirit creature," but his material body remained behind.) But Christians believe this. It is in fact integral to Christianity. You cannot have Christianity without Jesus's bodily resurrection.

So we probably can't stress the quality of the resurrection enough. Again, it is not a belief that Jesus revived or resuscitated. Neither is the resurrection the belief that Jesus only appeared to come back, as if he were a ghost or apparition of some kind. No, Jesus was physically, materially present in the world after his resurrection, but his body was different. It was changed, *glorified*. This meant that Jesus could be heard and touched. It meant that he could eat meals with his disciples and hold their hands. But it also meant that he could apparently walk through locked doors. It meant that sometimes he looked just like he did before and other times he looked mysteriously different. It meant that he could ascend right into heaven and live there in his glorified incarnate state.

Today, Christians do not simply worship Jesus out of sentimental memory or religious admiration, but out of committed belief that he is actually alive and that we who

2. Shai Linne, "Jesus Is Alive," *The Atonement* album (Lamp Mode, 2008), http://lampmode.com/the-atonement-lyrics/. Reprinted by permission.

are united to him by faith will enjoy resurrections of our own, just like his.

One of the most credible evidences we have for the historicity of Jesus Christ's resurrection is the sheer number of witnesses. From the women at the tomb to the early disciples to the great number of witnesses Paul cites in 1 Corinthians 15, there were people at the time of Jesus's ascension who could testify that they had actually seen him. You could go interview these people, which is, I think, why Paul mentions them. He knows this is an incredible claim, so he wants to make clear that there were witnesses who could certainly be questioned.

One of the earliest witnesses of Jesus's resurrection was John, perhaps Jesus's closest friend, occasionally called the disciple "whom Jesus loved" (John 13:23). After Christ's ascension, John got to see Jesus one more time before his own death. It was while he was exiled on the island of Patmos, and the vision John had of the glorified messiah is detailed in the biblical book of Revelation.

In this revelation, John sees Jesus in his heavenly splendor. The encounter is extraordinarily beautiful and stirring:

> When I saw him, I fell at his feet as though dead. But he laid his right hand on me, saying, "Fear not, I am the first and the last, and the living one. I died, and behold I am alive forevermore, and I have the keys of Death and Hades." (Rev. 1:17–18)

Now, Jesus is making three major claims in these words to John. He is telling us what he's done, who he is, and—based on what he's done and who he is—how we ought to respond.

The Resurrection Is the Turning Point to History

We'll take a look at the historical claim first. It's rather straightforward but it has astounding implications. Jesus says this: "I died, and behold I am alive forevermore."

This is actually the essence of the gospel message that is intrinsic to Christianity: the historical news that Jesus died and rose again. It is why in 1 Corinthians 15:20, Paul says, "But in fact Christ has been raised from the dead."

Paul says "in fact" to plant a stake in the historical timeline. "This happened," he states. And not simply in a spiritual way, but in a physical, historical, real way. Jesus was raised from the dead.

It is incredibly common today to hear people claim that the Christian view of Christ's resurrection is not all that unique. From news magazines and cable TV documentaries to the new atheist bloggers and progressive religionists, many people are claiming that the early Christians' belief in a resurrected Jesus owed more to pagan myths than to reality. But are these criticisms warranted?

The claim that Christianity's resurrection story is simply drawn from the "resurrection myths" of pagan religions has largely taken hold at the popular level of discourse, in the media and online. But when you get down to the actual myths Christianity is supposedly borrowing from, you actually find that there aren't many similarities at all.

Most of the claims of parallels made, typically shared in glossy "meme" images posted around social media, aren't even accurate. Perhaps you've seen the comparison between the myth of Horus and the Christmas story? In it the charge is made that Horus was born of a virgin, walked on water, healed the sick, was crucified, and then resurrected. But only one of these plot points occurs in the actual Horus story (healing the sick). The others are either outright fabrications or gross distortions of the narrative. (For instance, somehow Horus being the product of Isis and Osiris translates to a virgin birth.)

Over and over again, we see that the "pagan myth parallels" begin to fall under the weight of the actual narratives. Most of these claims get the myths entirely wrong. (No, neither Mithra nor Krishna died and was resurrected.) Others make huge leaps to find any connection that seems plausible.

In fact, most of the alleged parallels between Christianity's resurrection story and pagan myths could just as easily include every account of supernatural transcendence or spirituality. There really is no single story that resembles what the early Christians claimed happened to Jesus.

The ancient pagans and the religionists even of Jesus's day and after did not believe in resurrection. They put some things in their stories that sometimes stretched belief in the afterlife—people entering the underworld, people ascending to the heavens—but they didn't claim these things actually happened. But what Christians claimed about Jesus was unprecedented. As N. T. Wright says about the ancient world:

> Death was all powerful. One could neither escape it in the first place nor break its power once it had come. The ancient world was thus divided into those who said that resurrection couldn't happen, though they might have

wanted it to, and those who said they didn't want it to happen, knowing that it couldn't anyway . . .

A great many things supposedly happened to the dead, but resurrection did not. The pagan world assumed it was impossible; the Jewish world believed it would happen eventually, but knew perfectly well that it had not done so yet. Jew and non-Jew alike heard the early Christians to be saying that it had happened to Jesus. They did not suppose the Christians were merely asserting that Jesus' soul had attained some kind of heavenly bliss or special status. They did not think Jesus' disciples were merely describing, with gross hyperbole, their regular feasts at his tomb.[3]

No, the resurrection of Jesus Christ is unparalleled in literature and in religion.

It is also a ludicrous notion that Jesus did not actually die but perhaps only "swooned." This claim hinges on the idea that the Romans weren't very good at something they'd spent years perfecting—executing people. The agony Jesus underwent from his scourging to the crucifixion itself was simply not survivable. His back was flayed to incredible blood loss. The heat and exhaustion and dehydration would have also taken a severe toll. The excruciating pain of the crucifixion, not just in the nails through his hands and feet but in the positioning of his body, prevented unlabored breathing. Those condemned to crosses often had their legs broken to prevent them from pushing up on their nailed feet in order to position their bodies to fill their lungs with air. Breaking the legs hastened suffocation.

3. N. T. Wright, *The Resurrection of the Son of God* (Minneapolis: Fortress, 2003), 82–83.

We think Jesus's legs were not broken, not out of Roman mercy but out of either the desire to prolong his pain or the acknowledgment that he was already dying.

The "swoon theory" would have us imagine that Jesus somehow survived all of this and then somehow exited his tomb unnoticed or turned up with his followers shortly thereafter looking no worse for wear.

No, Jesus didn't swoon. "Behold: I died," he says.

Of course there is no "proof" of the resurrection, just as there is no "proof" that the United States had a president named Abraham Lincoln. What we have, though, is evidence. Credible evidence.

We have credible evidence that there was no precedent for this kind of belief before Christians started believing it. We know that Jews would not worship a man unless they really believed he was God, and they certainly would not have worshiped a dead man unless they believed he wasn't dead. We know that the historical account records women as the first witnesses to Jesus's empty tomb, which would have been the first mistake of any perpetrated fiction, as in the sexist culture of those days women were not considered reliable witnesses. We know that Jesus's body was never produced. We know that there were more than five hundred witnesses to the resurrected Jesus (1 Cor. 15:6). We know that these early Jews would not have gone to their own deaths for a claim they knew to be a lie. And we cannot account for the explosive growth of the early church, much less the conversion of people like Saul of Tarsus, unless a real vision of the risen Jesus had taken place.

If you put all of this together and more, it is, in my estimation, harder *not* to believe.

No, Jesus really died, really was buried, really rose again, and then ascended into heaven where he reigns both bodily and glorified, both incarnate and omnipresent. This is the historical claim Jesus makes in Revelation 1:17–18.

The Resurrection Is Audacious

But Jesus also makes an extremely bold claim about himself in John's vision. "I am the first and the last."

This is the kind of thing the religious leaders of his day wanted to stone him for. It is similar to the moment during his ministry when he says, "Before Abraham was, I am" (John 8:58). Jesus is here claiming the divine name—I AM. He is asserting his deity. He is proclaiming his God-ness.

That Jesus is testifying to his own deity should be seen as the direct result of his resurrection, because while the handful of raisings of the dead during his ministry needed a third party—namely, Jesus—to carry them out, Jesus doesn't need anyone to order him to "come forth." He comes forth of his own volition.

"I am alive forevermore" (Rev. 1:18).

Another stunning "I AM" statement. Along with "I am the first and the last," this is a claim to eternality. The risen, ascended Christ is here asserting once again his deity.

I had a friend who was a Jehovah's Witness, and he had a very difficult time with my belief in the deity of Jesus Christ. He just couldn't get there. We were often looking at the same Bible verses, but he was seeing something else. Me? I can't get beyond the abundance of references to Jesus being God in the flesh.

Philippians 2 says he was in very nature God and equal to God. Colossians 2:9 says all the fullness of deity dwells in him bodily. In Titus 2:13 Jesus is called "God and Savior." In Hebrews 1:8 the Father calls Jesus "God." John 1:1 says Jesus created the world and that he was God. In John 5, the Jews understand that by calling God his Father, he is making himself equal with God. In John 10:30, Jesus says, "I and the Father are one," and it makes them want to stone him for blasphemy. When the disciple Thomas sees the resurrected Jesus, he cries out to him, "My Lord and my God!"

In John 14:6, Jesus claims to be the way, the truth, and the life.

Look, normal people don't say these kinds of things. Even religious leaders don't usually say such things. They are typically pointing to *a* way, to *some* truth. Jesus was directing all of this toward *himself*.

In Jesus's own estimation, he is the end-all, be-all. And Christians believe Jesus is the first and the last, just as he says he is.

- He is the great High Priest, surpassing all priests.
- He is the Good Shepherd, surpassing all shepherds.
- He is the great Judge, surpassing all judges.
- He is the King of kings, surpassing all kings.
- He is the Lord of lords, surpassing all earthly masters.
- He is the Bridegroom, surpassing all husbands.
- He is the Rabbi Christ, surpassing all preachers.

- He is the Alpha and Omega, the beginning and the end, surpassing all the best of everybody ever.

The major problem with contemporary scholars' approach to Jesus's resurrection is that they come to do the work of autopsy, not adoration. But Jesus Christ is the apex of all that is precious, the center of all that is glorious and delightful. He is the very point of existence. He is the Son of the living God, the Alpha and Omega, the first and the last who was and is and is to come.

"O come let us adore him!"—not scrutinize, utilize, or analyze him.

The personal claim the risen Jesus makes about himself is that he is the God of the universe and that he deserves our awe, our reverence, our worship, our love, and our devotion.

The Resurrection Is Personal

The third claim the risen Jesus makes in Revelation 1:17–18 is about how we ought to respond to what he's done and who he is as seen in the gospel storyline of these two verses.

Now, this is what I mean by "gospel storyline." The gospel is the good news that Jesus's death and resurrection provide salvation for all who will believe in him. So the *gospel storyline* is how we see this news reflected in a passage of Scripture (or even in a work of art or in our own lives): it usually follows these plot points—conviction/repentance, receiving God's pardon, deliverance into heaven.

Here's where the gospel storyline begins in this passage: When John first sees Jesus, he "[falls] at his feet as though dead" (v. 17). Why?

It's what sinners do when faced with Christ's glory for the first time.

At the end of Mark's Gospel, as the Marys come to the tomb and find it empty, the angel that is there says, "Don't be alarmed." But what do they do? They flee in fear. It says, "Trembling and astonishment had seized them" (Mark 16:8). When the angels first announce the incarnation, the shepherds have a similar reaction: "The glory of the Lord shone around them, and they were filled with great fear" (Luke 2:9). In Isaiah 6, when Isaiah is in the temple and the glory of the Lord fills the place, he becomes undone, crying out, "Woe is me! For I am lost" (v. 5). In Nehemiah 8, as Ezra and Nehemiah read the Law, the people weep.

All of these are examples of people viscerally experiencing Hebrews 10:31: "It is a fearful thing to fall into the hands of the living God."

When we see who we are in the light of who God is for the first time, the result is pure conviction, sometimes a sort of spiritual discombobulation that reveals our utter need and our total desperation apart from God. You may not be an emotional person, but you can't be saved if you don't see that you're lost. If you don't see your need to be saved, you won't come to Christ for salvation. If you can't see that you are a sinner who deserves the wrath of God, you won't repent and receive his forgiveness.

So John sees the glory of his old friend Jesus, and he falls down in penitence. That's the first plot point in the gospel storyline.

But what does Jesus do? He puts his hand on him and says, "Fear not."

There's the second plot point in the gospel storyline—the welcome of grace.

When we come to Christ in reverence and repentance, he doesn't brush us off or kick us around. He welcomes us. He embraces us. He responds to our fear with words of peace and comfort. "Come to Me, all who are weary and heavy-laden," Jesus says in Matthew 11:28, "and I will give you rest" (NASB).

"Do not be afraid," Jesus says. "I am the first and the last, and the living One; and I was dead, and behold, I am alive forevermore, and I have the keys of death and of Hades" (Rev. 1:17–18 NASB).

We come in repentance and Jesus responds with forgiveness.

But the gospel story goes deeper than that. It is not simply about having sins forgiven and receiving a "ticket to heaven." Jesus, in making these claims about what he's done and who he is, receives those who seek forgiveness into a kingdom that is bigger than a blank slate and clean start.

And that is *the whole point* of the resurrection story. Heaven isn't just waiting "up there" for when people die. Heaven has come to earth. It is breaking into the very fabric of creation and rewiring the system with glorious restoration!

So we reach the third point in the gospel storyline: the gospel doesn't simply forgive our sins, it promises the gift of eternal life (John 3:16).

In his crucifixion and burial, Jesus goes right to the brokenness of the world itself, into death itself, and he dives straight into the destination and fear of every person—the grave and judgment—and he says, "I hold the keys."

Death and hell do not run rampant. They are not rogue elements in the fallen world. They are subject to the sovereignty of the one who controls and rules over them. Jesus has died, having received the condemnation of God's wrath on the cross, and he has come out the other side.

And he has done something extraordinary in dying and rising again, something peculiar to death and the grave itself. He didn't merely survive. He conquered!

Because of the resurrection of Jesus Christ, the Christian vision of death requires a radical overhaul, a redefinition. We think of death now as a kind of sleep, and we go from fearing death to actually *mocking* it (1 Cor. 15:55). Where do we get this authority, this position, this "arrogance" over death?

From Jesus Christ, who holds the keys to death and Hades, who says, "I died and I swallowed up death from the inside." I'm borrowing here from Jonathan Edwards, who once preached:

> The devil had, as it were, swallowed up Christ, as the whale did Jonah—but it was deadly poison to him, he gave him a mortal wound in his own bowels. He was soon sick of his morsel, and was forced to do by him as the whale did by

Jonah. To this day he is heart-sick of what he then swallowed as his prey.[4]

The grave swallowed Jesus, but Jesus made the grave so sick it had to vomit him out! And the grave has been sick ever since Christ's resurrection. Death ever since has been dying. Jesus holds its key.

This is what every human being has been longing for. We are doing everything we can to fight death, if we aren't trying to ignore it altogether. We fritter our time away with entertainment and other distractions. We work out, eat right, and take our vitamins. Deep down, we are desperately afraid of not existing anymore. But statistics show us that ten out of ten people who eat lots of kale *still die*. I'm sorry, but it's true.

And here comes Jesus Christ, defeating death. Conquering it. Taunting it. And then he turns around and offers this same ability to us, provided we trust in him. It turns out that our instinctive understanding that death is both natural and yet somehow unnatural is actually right!

Death reminds us that the world is not as it was meant to be. And the resurrection tells us that God's plans will not be thwarted forever.

"I died and I am alive forevermore." This is the resurrection made personal. To you. This is the invitational claim of the gospel, because you can say this too—"I died and I am alive forevermore"—if you will come to Jesus in faith, repenting of your sins and believing in him. You can be united to him through faith, to become as secure as he

4. Jonathan Edwards, "The Excellency of Christ," in *Sermons of Jonathan Edwards* (Peabody, MA: Hendrickson, 2005), 213.

is, so that his death becomes yours and his eternal life also becomes yours.

The Bible says, "If you confess with your mouth that Jesus is Lord and believe in your heart that God raised him from the dead, you will be saved" (Rom. 10:9).

But to have this triumph over death you must not see yourself as "over" the gospel. It must not be beneath you.

If we will say, "I can't do this. I can't manage this. I can't save myself. I need you, God. I want you, God. Forgive me, God. Receive me, God," we can hear by God's grace the full assurance of Christ in his welcome: "Fear not."

+   +   +   +   **8**   +

The Most Incredible Idea in the History of the Universe

HOW THE CHRISTIAN VIEW OF SALVATION IS UNIQUE AND INCOMPARABLE

Having served in various capacities in ministry for more than twenty years, I have had my fair share of religious conversations. And there's a dynamic in these conversations that occurs so often, it reminds me that the functional ideology of the entire world is a kind of legalism. Basically, most human beings believe that there are "good people" and "bad people." And what I find interesting is that most people believe they are good, and are ready to prove their goodness should the occasion demand it. But if it doesn't, they actually don't find it all that pressing.

Sometimes this turn happens on a dime.

I once met a man who spent a very long time telling me all about himself before ever asking whom he was talking to. Before I could get any word in edgewise, I'd learned more about him than I ever hoped to know. We weren't really in a conversation. He talked; I listened. He told me how he'd just been in New York on business but was looking forward to going back to Las Vegas, where he had recently been with a lady friend. I won't recount all the sordid details of his adventures there, but they involved lots of alcohol, gambling, and the Playboy suite at their hotel.

This is not the kind of conversation I hoped to have with anyone, much less a stranger who didn't realize he was in an impromptu counseling session with a pastor! I would have found the whole thing pathetic if he'd been a college-aged kid. But this was a grown man who should've known better than to try to impress me with his sleazy life.

It wasn't until after he'd told me all this that he finally got around to asking what everybody always asks: "So, what do you do?"

I told him.

Silence.

I don't remember how he made the transition. All I know is that he didn't stop his attempt to impress me. He simply tried to impress me with something else. He began to list out some good works. I remember mostly him telling me about giving to needy folks in New Orleans after Hurricane Katrina. He also said something about helping single mothers at Christmastime buy gifts for their kids.

What happened?

The guy had discovered I was a "religious person," a religious *professional* even, and he suddenly became self-conscious about all the sketchy stuff with which he'd tried to earn my approval. Now he was listing out some good works so I wouldn't get the "wrong idea." He's not so bad after all. He's really a good guy. He's "spiritual, but not religious."

I don't know if he wanted me to grant him an official pardon or what. I couldn't understand what he hoped to gain from me in way of conversation after hearing of all his good deeds.

In the end I asked him what I ask all those trying to game the system with the weight of their own righteousness: "What do you think the message of Christianity is?"

He didn't know.

And that's when I blew his mind with the most radical idea in the history of the universe. Christians call this idea *grace.*

Grace Is the Essence of Christianity

I'm not sure the average Christian quite understands how essential grace is to Christianity. It is the very central idea, coming from the very center of Jesus Christ himself. It is so essential to Christianity, in fact, that if you lose grace, you lose Christianity. Paul writes this in Romans 11:5–6:

So too at the present time there is a remnant, chosen by grace. But if it is by grace, it is no longer on the basis of works; otherwise grace would no longer be grace.

He is making basically two claims here in the midst of his letter to the Romans. The first is that anyone who is a believer is not a believer because of their good works. They are, in fact, "chosen by grace." So if someone is a Christian, they may be known by their works of love, yet they didn't become a Christian by their works of love but rather by God's work of love in Jesus Christ. Christians become Christians *by grace*. Secondly, because of this truth, Paul is saying that if you piggyback any good works into the equation of salvation, you lose the very foundation of grace. "Grace would no longer be grace," he says. If you dilute or compromise the grace, you lose it.

And, again, if you lose the grace, you lose the whole of Christianity.

But what is grace?

Grace has been commonly defined as "unmerited favor," and that's a fine enough definition. Grace is the giving of a blessing apart from an earning of the blessing. The idea of grace in Christianity corresponds to the notion that God saves sinners purely because he loves them and therefore wants to save them. He does not save them because they've been good enough to somehow merit his interest. Real, authentic Christianity teaches that only Jesus Christ is able to do the impossible work of justifying sinners before a perfect and holy God.

Therefore, when Christians talk about salvation by grace, they eventually have to talk about this idea in Romans 11:5

of being "chosen by grace." There's no way of getting around it. Any way you slice it, even if you get it really thin, to base our salvation on any act of our own is to dilute the potency of grace involved.

In his book *A Brief History of Time*, physicist Stephen Hawking, considered by some to be the smartest man in the world, shared this well-traveled anecdote:

> A well-known scientist (some say it was Bertrand Russell) once gave a public lecture on astronomy. He described how the earth orbits around the sun and how the sun, in turn, orbits around the center of a vast collection of stars called our galaxy. At the end of the lecture, a little old lady at the back of the room got up and said: "What you have told us is rubbish. The world is really a flat plate supported on the back of a giant tortoise." The scientist gave a superior smile before replying, "What is the tortoise standing on?" "You're very clever, young man, very clever," said the old lady. "But it's turtles all the way down!"[1]

According to Christian theology, what is the ratio of grace to works in the salvation equation? 1 to 0. Not one speck, not one microgram, not one atom of works there. It is all grace or no grace. Wring and wrestle all you want, but it is grace *all the way down*.

Grace is essential to authentic Christianity. And this is the first reason grace is the most radical idea in the history of the universe and makes Christianity utterly unique.

1. Stephen Hawking, *A Brief History of Time* (New York: Bantam, 1998), 1.

Grace Is the Only Basis of Salvation

Christianity teaches this: if you don't have grace, you aren't saved.

When you boil it all down, this is the thing that distinguishes the Christian religion from every other religion and philosophy in the world. Christianity has a few things in common with every religious ideology and more things in common with a few specific religions (such as Judaism or Islam), but there is one thing that only Christianity has, the thing that makes it utterly unique. That thing is the gospel of Jesus Christ.

Now, you may ask, the message of Jesus certainly makes Christianity *Christianity*, but every religion has the message of its own founder or guru or divine leader particular to itself, doesn't it? But that is not what we mean when we say the gospel makes Christianity unique. The gospel makes Christianity unique among all other religions and philosophical systems of enlightenment, approval, or success because while every other system primarily teaches *things to do*, only Christianity primarily teaches that the things to do are *done*.

Outside of Christianity, both religious and irreligious systems aimed at personal success or fulfillment hold out for their adherents a certain goal—heaven, nirvana, reincarnation, enlightenment, happiness, and so forth—and then list out a set of steps or instructions to reach that goal. In religious systems, the steps are steps of obedience, commandments that must be followed to reach the stated goal. Christianity has steps of obedience too, of course. Christianity teaches that the God of the Bible is holy and just and that his commandments are meant to be obeyed. But only Christianity teaches that the human ability to obey God's commandments in a way that would merit salvation simply doesn't exist. We can't do it.

Other religions may talk about God forgiving us for our sins, but the way to receive that forgiveness entails a certain level of obedience, as well. We must earn forgiveness. Christianity, rightly understood, teaches that we cannot earn forgiveness. We aren't good enough. Even our best deeds are tainted by wrong motivations, and even our best intentions result in imperfect obedience.

U2 singer Bono has said some interesting things about the distinction between Christian teaching and literally every other religion and philosophy:

> The thing that keeps me on my knees is the difference between Grace and Karma . . . You see, at the center of all religions is the idea of Karma. You know, what you put out comes back to you: an eye for an eye, a tooth for a tooth, or in physics—in physical laws—every action is met by an equal or an opposite one. It's clear to me that Karma is at the very heart of the universe. I'm absolutely sure of it. And yet, along comes this idea called Grace to upend all that "as you reap, so you will sow" stuff. Grace defies reason and logic. Love interrupts, if you like, the consequences of your actions, which in my case is very good news indeed, because I've done a lot of stupid stuff.[2]

He has hit on the ultimate truth of human existence, the very truth that makes the difference between living and

2. "Bono: Grace over Karma," *Christianity Today* (August 1, 2005), http://www
.christianitytoday.com/ct/2005/augustweb-only/bono-0805.html?paging=off.

dying, between salvation and judgment. If you're trusting in yourself, you are in real trouble. Bono goes on to say this:

> I'd be in big trouble if Karma was going to finally be my judge. I'd be in deep s—. It doesn't excuse my mistakes, but I'm holding out for Grace. I'm holding out that Jesus took my sins onto the Cross, because I know who I am, and I hope I don't have to depend on my own religiosity.[3]

Yes! You don't have to depend on your religiosity!

So how do we get this interruption? How do we get delivered from the condemnation of karma? It does not come from within. It comes in the form of divine rescue in the message Bono has just identified as "good news." The apostle Paul expresses the good news of divine rescue this way in 1 Corinthians 15:1–4:

> Now I would remind you, brothers, of the gospel I preached to you, which you received, in which you stand, and by which you are being saved, if you hold fast to the word I preached to you—unless you believed in vain.
>
> For I delivered to you as of first importance what I also received: that Christ died for our sins in accordance with the Scriptures, that he was buried, that he was raised on the third day in accordance with the Scriptures.

The gospel is the good news that our loving God, in an act of sheer grace, sent his Son Jesus to live the sinless life we should've lived and accept as punishment for sin the death we would've died. Jesus died on the cross as a perfect, willing sacrifice in our place. Further, he then rose from the grave in

---

3. Ibid.

a living, glorified body to secure for us the promise of eternal life and our own future resurrection in a glorified state. The gospel is the announcement, then—the good news—that God saves sinners by his grace given in the completed work of Jesus, totally apart from the sinners' works of obedience.

Because the gospel is what distinguishes Christianity from every other religion and philosophy, it should be the message we consider the most important. Paul himself calls the gospel "of first importance" in 1 Corinthians 15:3. This means that the gospel is the most important thing about Christianity, and thus ought to be held as the most important thing in Christian churches.

Thus Paul's logic in Romans 11:6—if salvation is by grace, it cannot be by works, because if it's by works, it's no longer grace, and if it's no longer grace, it's no longer Christianity.

The "remnant" in Romans 11:5 speaks to the elect, those whom God has chosen to receive the blessing of the gospel of Jesus Christ. Out of all the people in the world, he has kept a people to himself and for himself. He sets his grace upon them; in fact he set his grace upon them before the world was even created, and when the fullness of time has come, the fullness of grace comes and does its saving work. And this leads us to the second reason grace is so amazing, the thing that makes grace no ordinary religious idea.

Grace Is Powerful

The remnant Paul speaks about in Romans 11:5–6 is chosen by grace, and the remnant is saved by grace, and the remnant is *sustained* by grace.

Clearly, grace runs deeper than simply inspiring a conversion experience.

See, the importance of distinguishing between works and grace in Christian teaching is not simply to distinguish the doctrines and definitions but to distinguish what actually works to transform people and what doesn't. And so the corollary claim to grace in Christian doctrine is equally provocative: *commandments have no power*.

Another thing we notice in 1 Corinthians 15:1–4 is a rather peculiar bit of information about this information we call the gospel. The gospel is news, yes, but it appears to be more than just mere data. It's like a newspaper headline—"Son of God Dies for the Sins of the World"—but it does things no other newspaper headline could ever do.

In 1 Corinthians 15:1, we see that we "receive" this news. But we also see in verse 2 that we "stand" in it and that it is somehow saving us in an ongoing way. Clearly, this is no ordinary news! What we learn in the Bible is that the gospel of Jesus Christ is *powerful*. It is a power in and unto itself.

In Romans 1:16, Paul writes, "For I am not ashamed of the gospel, for it is the *power* of God for salvation" (emphasis added). In Ephesians 3:7 Paul says the gospel was given to him by God's power. In 1 Thessalonians 1:5 he says the gospel is accompanied by power.

So we see that the good news of grace isn't just power enough for our conversion ("you received") but for the ongoing declaration of our definitive justification ("in which you stand") and the progressive sanctifying work we are undergoing and future glorification we will enjoy in heaven ("by which you are being saved").

It is important to think about the gospel this way, not just because this is what the Bible teaches about the gospel but because it helps us distinguish the gospel's power from the law's power. In our churches too often we believe the way people change is by receiving more instruction. Instruction is good, and we need it. There are lots of instructions in the Bible, and we shouldn't ignore them. But the way the Bible says people actually change, deep down in the heart, where the sincerity is seated that makes our behavior worship of God instead of worship of self, is by believing in the gospel.

In 2 Corinthians 3:18 Paul says that it is by beholding the glory of Jesus Christ that we are transformed "from one degree of glory to another." Truly "seeing" Christ in the gospel as supreme and satisfying and saving is what empowers us to worship him. The law cannot do that!

You can no sooner get life change out of the law than you can raise the dead by cracking a whip over a corpse. You need power, and only God's grace has resurrection power.

But we do the logic of the law and think it works the other way. And so does everybody else. We know how people change—we just tell them to get their act together! But do you know what will change the world? Not complaining! Every day on Facebook our friends and families link to article after article of opposing political and religious demagoguery and *nobody ever changes their mind.*

Certainly nobody ever changes their heart because they were told to behave differently.

So while every other religion and philosophy in the world says change comes from within and "salvation" (however it's defined) is achieved by the right behaviors, only

Christianity teaches that real change comes from outside of ourselves and that salvation is achieved by Christ's behavior.

Please note that this is not the same thing as saying people shouldn't change their behavior. Do the Christian Scriptures command people to obey? Yes. Are there demands upon our life in service of God's kingdom? Yes. And the enduring law of commandments, which is good, provides our blueprint for what life built in worship of God looks like. But the law itself is not able to supply what it demands.

The law will not change a heart; the law will not cure the idolatry at the root of every disobedience. In fact, in Titus 2:11–12 Paul says that it is *grace*, not the law, that trains us to "act right."

The startling reality is this: the gospel empowers its own implications. Where the law of religion says "Get to work," the gospel of grace says "It. Is. Finished."

In saving us powerfully, grace has set us free from the curse of the law, the bondage of sin, and the idolatry of the self. And what happens when you're set free?

You cheer, you run, you dance, you sing. Here, then, is another reason grace is the most incredible idea in the history of the universe.

Only Grace Provokes Real Worship of God

The law can provoke adherence, behavior modification, conformity. But because it cannot get at the heart, it cannot provoke real, authentic, sincere worship. You see this in other religions that promote law-based adherence to the teaching: they don't sing like Christians sing.

I notice this most significantly at funerals. In my capacity as pastor I have had the opportunity to officiate more memorial services than I can count. I have preached the funerals of both believers and unbelievers. Part of the funeral preparations always involves asking about music. When a non-Christian family chooses music for their loved one's service, they typically go right to the only hymn they know, the most famous hymn in the world of hymns. You know exactly which one I'm talking about.

But unbelievers sing "Amazing Grace" much differently than believers. When Christians sing, "How sweet the sound that saved a wretch like me," they feel it. When they sing, "I once was lost but now I'm found," they mean it.

Christians who understand the radical reality of grace don't mumble through hymns like this. They don't chant these songs. They don't yawn through the lines about rescue and redemption and reverence. The music comes from the bottom of their souls, from the marrow of their bones, from the bottoms of their feet to the tops of their invisible crowns. I know this may be controversial to say, but I'll say it again: nobody sings like Christians.

Pastor and author John Piper reflects this way:

> I don't think there are any other religions that sing like Christians sing. Christians really make music over their faith.
>
> Even the sheer radio reality of Christian contemporary music is an interesting phenomenon. It has many pitfalls because of, perhaps, the way that theology is dumbed down in it or the way it is infected with an entertainment mindset; but the sheer existence of Christians who are always

looking for ways to make melody about their faith—finding inspiring tunes growing out of their convictions about God and Christ and forgiveness and eternal life—I think that is an amazing and unique thing. I don't think there are any other faiths in the world that come close.

In fact some faiths, like Islam, don't even believe in singing. But what kind of faith could say that the human heart, with its readiness to make melody over almost everything it enjoys, should not do that over the most important reality in the universe? That's a really strange religion, I think.[4]

Christians exult. Christians revel. Christians relish. Christians adore. That's not the same thing as just singing.

And see, you can't get adoration of God from the self-help gobbledygook on religious TV or from the inspirational bobbleheads on the talk shows with their bland fortune cookie pep talks. Christianity is resurrection business.

And you don't get resurrection from moralistic platitudes but instead from the Spirit of grace. And part of this reveling in grace is seeing how much of it there is!

In Titus 2:11, Paul writes, "For the grace of God has appeared, bringing salvation for all people." That Greek word behind the phrase "has appeared" is *epiphaneia*. It's the same word we get our English word *epiphany* from. It's a revelation. Grace has appeared! Somebody has finally turned the lights on.

This would be our perception of grace if we could see just how versatile and abundant it is. In 2 Corinthians 12:9,

4. John Piper, "Why Is Singing So Important for Christians?" *Desiring God* (September 14, 2007), http://www.desiringgod.org/interviews/why-is-singing -so-important-for-christians.

we read, "But he said to me, 'My grace is sufficient for you.'" Grace is enough. In 1 Corinthians 15:10, we see that Paul's work is the result of the grace of God inside of him, so we see that grace is power. In 2 Timothy 2:1, we read, "You then, my child, be strengthened by the grace that is in Christ Jesus," so we see that grace is strength. In 2 Corinthians 4:15, we read, "For it is all for your sake, so that as grace extends to more and more people it may increase thanksgiving, to the glory of God," so we see that grace produces thankfulness.

In Colossians 4:6, we read, "Let your speech always be gracious, seasoned with salt, so that you may know how you ought to answer each person," so we see that grace changes the way we talk. In 2 Corinthians 1:12, we read, "For our boast is this, the testimony of our conscience, that we behaved in the world with simplicity and godly sincerity, not by earthly wisdom but by the grace of God, and supremely so toward you," so we see that grace changes the way we live.

And in John 1:16, we read that "from his fullness"—that is, from Christ's fullness—we receive "grace upon grace," so we see that in Christ, grace is ever-flowing, always-filling, never-ending. And this brings us to the most incredible truth about the most incredible idea in the history of the universe. Grace is the most amazing because it gives us the most amazing Person that exists.

Grace Transfers Christ to Us

If we are not saved on the basis of works, what saves us? God's grace. And this grace comes to us in the declaration of God considering Jesus's good behavior as our good behavior. That idea alone is enough to blow up the tidy moral calculus of every other way of living. But there is something even deeper about the gospel, in the Bible's teaching about God's grace for sinners, that cannot be ignored.

Christianity is a spiritual enterprise. It is a supernatural thing, and what the gospel announces to us is that the God who has justified us is *sanctifying* us. What that means is he is cleansing us. He isn't content to just declare us clean; he means to *actually* make us clean. He is making us, bit by bit, more and more like his Son Jesus Christ. He is by his own power transforming us into the image of Christ.

And so this grace that transforms us is not some ethereal, magic fairy dust. It is—get this—actually Jesus! Grace is Jesus himself.

Pastor and scholar Sinclair Ferguson writes:

> It is legitimate to speak of "receiving grace," and sometimes (although I am somewhat cautious about the possibility of misusing this language) we speak of the preaching of the Word, prayer, baptism, and the Lord's Supper as "means of grace." That is fine, so long as we remember that there isn't a thing, a substance, or a "quasi-substance" called "grace." All there is is the person of the Lord Jesus—"Christ clothed in the gospel," as John Calvin loved to put it. Grace is the grace of Jesus. If I can highlight the thought here: there is no "thing" that Jesus takes from Himself and then, as it were, hands over to me. There is only Jesus Himself. Grasping that thought can make a significant difference to a Christian's life. So while some people might think this is just splitting hairs about different ways of saying the same

thing, it can make a vital difference. It is not a thing that was crucified to give us a thing called grace. It was the person of the Lord Jesus that was crucified in order that He might give Himself to us through the ministry of the Holy Spirit.[5]

So the wonder for sinners stuck in the murky limbo of moral karma is that in receiving the gospel, we receive Christ—all of him for all of us—not a bit of him held back from us, and we are united to him, and we are conformed to his image, and he intercedes for us and is our eternal advocate. He covers us in his righteousness, and the more deeply we press into our identity in Christ, the more we naturally—which is to say, *supernaturally*—become like him.

Praise God for his marvelous grace! His grace that hi jacks us and waylays us and apprehends us and transforms us and transfers to us the very Lord of Creation himself, Jesus Christ.

When we diminish the realities of salvation by Christ and insist on smuggling our obedience into the equation, we diminish grace. As Paul says, "otherwise grace would no longer be grace."

If you are a follower of Jesus, then, it is important that you not disgrace grace by treating Christianity like a list of instructions or commandments. Christianity is not essentially about the Bible's to-do lists. It is essentially about Christ's "done" declaration.

5. Nathan W. Bingham, "By Grace Alone: An Interview with Sinclair Ferguson," Ligonier Ministries (June 6, 2014), http://www.ligonier.org/blog/grace-alone-interview-sinclair-ferguson/.

And isn't that a more compelling message? Sure, not everyone will think so. Not everyone will get the appeal. It is a spiritual thing, salvation. We really do need the wonder of grace itself to wake us up to the wonder of grace itself.

But for so many locked into the karmic treadmill of "do more, try harder, be better," doesn't this message called the good news stand out? There's nothing like it. You can't get this anywhere else. While everybody else is demanding obedience, Christianity is pointing to the obedience of Christ. It is—because *he* is—our only hope.

We need him. We need his perfect, spotless righteousness. We need his intervention. We need his merciful hand. We need his friendship with sinners. We need his abounding love. We need his amazing grace. Or else we die.

We need Christ because, even if we have all the merit badges in the world, all the successes and the trophies and the adulation and the education, if we do not have Christ, we have nothing.

9

Have News, Will Travel

HOW CHRISTIAN MISSION
IS COMPELLING AND CONTAGIOUS

There seemed to be some sort of cultural tipping point in religious perspectives around the time of the Hurricane Katrina disaster along America's Gulf Coast in 2005. The nation was tossed into political upheaval, as well, as nightly news broadcasts showed us the toll the storm and ensuing floods had taken on poorer communities, where the number of deaths was higher and the government response seemed slower. But this tragedy, in my mind, coincided with a larger shift in American public discourse on the place of religion in society.

Cultural Christianity had already been crumbling for some time. The equation of "conservative Christian" with "narrow-minded bigot" had already become commonplace. But somehow in the response to the disaster, Christians took a pretty hard licking.

I blame Sean Penn.

Okay, not really. But I vividly remember Sean Penn in his little boat with his camera crew, tooling around the floodwaters looking for people to be the savior of. And I'm probably making a huge leap to see a correlation here, but it just seemed like one more example of the liberal celebrity messiah complex (see also George Clooney and Oprah Winfrey) making us look bad. In the blogosphere those days, evangelicals took a lot of heat for not caring about hurricane victims like Hollywood's elite did.

It was maddening. Because I knew Christians were caring for hurricane victims in far greater numbers than these Hollywood celebrities. The main difference is that Christians usually help without taking a camera crew along.

We will also often hear, particularly out of the new atheism championed by Christopher Hitchens and Richard Dawkins, that religion in general and Christianity in particular are largely responsible for so much of the pain and injustice in the world. And while it is true that religious people are not exempt from the sin that infects every human being, these claims are rather specious. They seem to make no allowance for the most brutal and unjust political regimes throughout world history, which have mostly been atheistic. They also don't seem to account for the fact that religious folks had been caring for the poor, the sick, and the hungry on a large-scale effort for hundreds of years before the new atheists thought to complain about them.

Do we have a long way to go? Yes.

Are we self-centered, self-interested, and self-involved? Well, often.

But the image of the stingy American church is essentially a false one. (It particularly irks me when the criticism of outside celebrities and even younger church leaders makes it sound like they invented missions and charity ten years ago.)

Douglas Wilson has a revealing and penetrating perspective:

> Americans are about six percent of the world's population and we account for about forty-five percent of the world's philanthropy. Among Americans, believers are far more generous than secularists. Among believers, Protestants are more liberal in their giving than Catholics. Among Protestants, evangelicals are more generous than mainliners. But if you were [to] ask a secular arbiter of all that is philanthropic for his opinion on how we were doing, he would invert the whole thing.[1]

Survey after survey continues to show, also, that those who identify with political conservatism dramatically outgive in charitable contributions those who identify as liberal. Of course, that is not a religious survey, but perhaps

---

1. Douglas Wilson, "The Dry Hole of Secular Leftism," *Blog and Mablog* (August 14, 2008), http://dougwils.com/s7-engaging-the-culture/the-dry-hole-of-secular-leftism.html.

the correlation can be forgiven if we can acknowledge that the group most often denigrated for their apathy and stinginess—evangelical Christians—is also the group most likely to identify with conservative politics.

The truth is that nobody out-serves or out-gives evangelical Christians worldwide. We just don't host telethons.

How Christianity Grows

Christian mission has always thrived by surging in the margins and under the radar. When we somehow get into positions of power, the wheels always come off. This is pretty much the way it's always been. I once heard Steve Brown relate this story on the radio: "A Muslim scholar once said to a Christian, 'I cannot find anywhere in the Quran that it teaches Muslims how to be a minority presence in the world. And I cannot find anywhere in the New Testament where it teaches Christians how to be a majority presence in the world.'"

Indeed, as Christianity spread throughout the first few centuries as a persecuted minority people, it was the conversion of Constantine that paved the way for its becoming the official state religion of the Roman Empire by the end of the fourth century. That's quite a turnaround for some backwater sect splintering off an oppressed Palestinian Judaism. But as my old religion professor in college, M. B. Jackson, used to say, "When everyone's a Christian, no one is." And once Christianity became the official religion, the church lost its prophetic voice and its vibrancy.

Many religions, like Islam for example, seem to thrive on conquest and power. Christianity grows best under hardship. There are more Christians in China today, for instance, where free expression of faith is illegal, than the total population of the United States. Christianity is in decline in America and Christendom is already in ruins in Europe, but in the East and in Africa, where it is new, a grassroots movement, and/or under persecution, it is spreading like wildfire.

I sometimes wonder if God has set the growth of Christianity to work this way to keep in the forefront of our minds the treasure and glory of heaven over and above the treasure and glory of earth.

Jesus sets the tone for Christians' quiet mission this way:

> Beware of practicing your righteousness before other people in order to be seen by them, for then you will have no reward from your Father who is in heaven. Thus, when you give to the needy, sound no trumpet before you, as the hypocrites do in the synagogues and in the streets, that they may be praised by others. Truly, I say to you, they have received their reward. But when you give to the needy, do not let your left hand know what your right hand is doing, so that your giving may be in secret. And your Father who sees in secret will reward you. (Matt. 6:1–4)

Unlike other religions, where good works are central to success, Christianity proclaims the glory of Jesus Christ and his work, and the good works of his followers become the beautiful dust stirred up in our following him wherever he goes. Christians are not earning their salvation with their good deeds; they are working it out (Phil. 2:12). And since Christians believe that the work of salvation is already accomplished by Jesus and that there is nothing left for them to do to contribute to this work, they are now free to unselfconsciously love and serve others without worrying about recognition or reward. They will be vindicated in heaven, even if they are violated here.

Christians are called to good works. This is how people know we are Christians. But they also know we are Christians—and not charitable Buddhists—because we don't make good works our boast.

The Place of Good Works

So what is the good place of good works in the life of Christian mission? How should we think of them if not as ways to earn God's love or pay our debt? Paul tells us something very provocative in Ephesians 2:8–10:

> For by grace you have been saved through faith. And this is not your own doing; it is the gift of God, not a result of works, so that no one may boast. For we are his workmanship, created in Christ Jesus for good works, which God prepared beforehand, that we should walk in them.

Now, the order of the salvation event presented here is crucially important. Christians believe that we are saved *by* grace received *through* faith. Grace precedes faith, because, as Ephesians 2:1–4 pointed out for us, apart from the intervention of God, we aren't just religiously disabled, we are dead. And we are saved by God's grace, "not as a result of works."

So to understand where works fit into the Christian life, we have to really understand grace. Hopefully you understand it a little better after chapter 8. But the point Paul makes here, which he also makes hundreds of other times, all over his letters, is that we are not saved because we made something of ourselves. We are not saved because we work harder than anybody else. And we are not saved because we follow the Christian religion.

Christians are saved because God saved them. We are *his* workmanship, not ours.

Now, the verse that says this also says we are "created in Christ Jesus for good works." So works are not incidental. And they aren't optional. We must obey God.

But here we learn that the God who created us for good works has also created these good works for us to do!

Let's get our feet under us, though. I keep coming back to this point because it is one of the most important tenets of Christianity that makes it totally unparalleled in the world, among systems both religious and irreligious: our good works do not earn us heaven.

See, there are two things that good works cannot be if they are ever to be what the Bible calls "good." They cannot be payback. And they cannot be self-righteous.

We do not work in order to pay God back. The debt is paid! This is what it means to be justified. No more payment is needed. Christians are not in debt to God; at least, not in this way. His Son has satisfied the payment.

In fact, elsewhere Paul says that we are not debtors but rather heirs (Rom. 8:12–17).

It's "good works as payback" that accounts for legalism and graceless religion and that spurs self-righteousness. If we treat our good works as payback, we'll burn out quickly, because we can never repay the infinite debt our sin has created. The glory of God is a huge and weighty thing. How arrogant we would be if we thought we could score some of it with some good deeds. We are not that good.

On the other hand, some of us think we're doing pretty well at the good works stuff. This is perhaps more dangerous than struggling to pay God back. Self-righteous works are the indicator that someone is very full of himself or herself. Self-righteous works are the works done to make ourselves look good, that we might get some glory. And this is a losing game, even though we often don't feel like we're losing.

I once had a guy come up to me at a conference and say he had repented of everything. He'd made a personal inventory of his heart, he'd asked God to help him see every sin he'd committed, and he'd repented of all of it, and now he had no sin left. "What do I do now?" he said. "I'm done repenting of my sins."

I said, "Well, I can think of one more for you."

He needed to repent of thinking he could ever stop repenting.

So if works cannot be payback and they cannot be self-righteous, what are they?

Two things: worship and warfare.

The good works that honor God are works done in delightful response to the finished work of Jesus Christ. It's not about payback; it's about praise. Good works are the resulting life of the heart that has been set free. And the more you know of the gospel, the freer you feel and the more your good works will be instinctual rather than dutiful. This is what Paul is getting at in Galatians 5 with all that talk about the fruit of the Spirit. Good works as worship is not about earning but about delighting.

In the psalms, David talks about delighting in God's law. It tastes like honey to him. How can he say that? Have you ever read God's law? I mean, have you read Leviticus lately? It's not sweet. It's heavy, burdensome, and kind of boring, honestly. How could he find it sweet?

Well, I think finding God's law sweet involves in some way feeling set free from it. And when we are set free *from* good works we realize we are set free *to* good works.

My God has set me free! Why *wouldn't* I follow and obey him?

But good works are also warfare. When God created Adam and Eve and told them to take dominion, they disobeyed and the whole plan got fractured.

Yet God has a plan for the coming ages. He is making all things new. He is not going to let sin get in the way of his plan for creation and the created order.

When Christians are brought into the kingdom of God, they are given the mandate to "take dominion" once again, not through physical or literal warfare but in the way of spiritual warfare. And while most of us think that spiritual warfare is about resisting the devil and casting out demons—and it is about that, to some extent—it's also about staking the claim of God's glory everywhere. And we do that through good works.

Good works are the signposts we build toward heaven. They point people upward. I mean, the same Jesus who said to keep your good works on the down low also said this: "In the same way, let your light shine before others, so that they may see your good works and give glory to your Father who is in heaven" (Matt. 5:16).

One of the most vivid illustrations of good works as both worship and warfare that I know of is found in the Old Testament story of David and Goliath. The Israelites and the Philistines square off in the Valley of Elah, and they agree to send their best fighters out to face each other rather than risk so much bloodshed among the armies. The Philistines send out their champion, Goliath. The Israelites have nobody, because they're all afraid. Until David, a shepherd and the future king of Israel, strides forth valiantly.

I'm sure you've heard the story of how he defeated Goliath with one stone hurled from his sling. The big man fell and died and thus Israel defeated the Philistines. And what did all those Israelites do? Now that the victory had been won for them, David's victory became their victory, and they plundered the enemy camp, whooping and hollering and exulting in the glory of a battle won without having to fight.

That's good works. It is plundering the enemy camp after the battle has been won for us.

And the great thing about good works for Christians is that they are guaranteed. No true Christian will fail to produce good deeds. God will not have any genuine believers who do not produce fruit. Good trees must produce good fruit (Matt. 7:17). That's what Paul's getting at in Ephesians

2:10 when he says, "God prepared [them] beforehand, that we should walk in them."

See, you thought your good works and your obedience were your idea! But, no, they were God's.

And this is okay. Don't get bummed out by this. I know some people hear this kind of thing and get offended, and think, *Am I some kind of robot, then?*

No, you're not a robot. Christians do good works by their own set-free will, but they couldn't do them unless God set them free to do them and ordained that they do them.

And this is good news. Why would you be mad about God ordaining your good works? It means that he gets the glory, not you. Are you mad about that?

Also, God ordaining your works means that you will actually produce good works! Guaranteed. He's going to prepare them for you. This means that if you are a true believer in Christ you *will* have them. How could you be mad about that?

And then, when you get to heaven, you will see all the good works God gave you to do and empowered you to do, polished and purified and stored up as an eternal treasure for you to enjoy. And when he ushers in the new heavens and the new earth, all the dominion we've taken by him and through him and for him with our good works will last forever as monuments to his glory in the earth.

But I'm getting ahead of myself. We're going to look at the new thing God is doing now and into the future in our next chapter. For now, though, I would strongly caution anyone who's irritated by the idea that God has ordained their obedience.

You do not want it any other way. Do not try bringing your own righteousness to the negotiating table with God. He will never strike a deal for it. In fact, the more of your works you try to offer up for his righteousness, the cheaper you make his righteousness look.

Bring nothing. Bring your emptiness. Bring your spiritual poverty. Bring your empty hands, your pockets pulled inside out. And if you come to Christ, owning the reality that *you have nothing* to offer him, he will give you eternity.

Christianity's Rapid Adaptability

When Jesus Christ ushered in the kingdom of God, announcing this gospel of his life, death, and resurrection to bring it to bear and make it available, he did so not just for his Jewish countrymen but for the non-Jew as well. This is something that the apostle Paul, himself a Jew, made his life's ambition to pursue—mission to the Gentiles.

It is God's goal, projected even in the Hebrew Scriptures, to unite every tongue, tribe, race, and nation under the banner of his sovereign glory revealed in Jesus Christ. And so it is the mission of the church to take this message everywhere, announcing the availability of forgiveness of sins and the eternality of life in Christ to people all over the globe, in every kind of nation, regardless of their ethnicity, their class, their religion, or their gender.

Over the last two thousand years, what we've discovered is that Christianity is remarkably good at this. And it is divinely well suited for it.

Islam has been making inroads into the West and in Africa, but it is still largely dominant only in the Middle East. Buddhism has an affiliate office in Hollywood, obviously, but it is still chiefly localized in the Far East. Ditto Confucianism. Hinduism mainly resides in India and Nepal. There are more Jews in America than in Israel, but they are only 2.2 percent of the American population. They are 75 percent of the population in Israel.

Only Christianity—begun by Jews localized in Jerusalem, later dominated by Greeks in the Mediterranean world, then centralized in Europe, then North America, and now, in terms of sheer numbers, "centralized" in China, Africa, and Latin America—has corporately gone on a global walkabout.

How can this be?

I think it is primarily because only Christianity teaches works-free justification.

There are religions in the world that compel a woman to travel hundreds of miles to kiss a statue, a man to walk across a wilderness to bathe in a sacred river, and men and women alike to crawl on their hands and knees. Every Muslim who is able must visit Mecca once before they die. It is required.

But there are no compulsory pilgrimages in Christianity, no far-flung hoops to jump through. The pilgrimage has been made: God incarnated in man. He comes to us in Spirit. Every religion, beside the true one, bids travel for power. In Christianity, power travels to us. The kingdom is not "out there." It is "in here." The temple is not "there." It's "here," because Christ tabernacles with us. The gospel that goes into the world and grows and bears fruit goes into the world when we do.

Because every real Christian has the true gospel, every real Christian is equipped for mission work at the time of their salvation. Have gospel, will travel! Christ goes where we go.

And there is also the great adaptability of Christianity. No, not of its truth claims. Christians don't fudge on the essential beliefs that make them Christians. When we talk about contextualizing the faith to different cultures, biblical Christians are not talking about compromising the faith. But with so many other religions being almost inextricably tied to specific tribal or national cultures, Christianity stands apart as especially nimble in the global age.

You will find vibrant Christian communities among a wide variety of people groups all over the world, and while their expressions and cultural characteristics will be all over the map, their essential beliefs will be on the same page. Christianity is amazingly adaptable. To become a Christian in Africa, you don't have to dress like a Christian in Atlanta. This is not always true for the spread of, for example, Islam, which typically comes with customary dress and the like.

Christians are also relentlessly devoted to translating the Bible into the tongue of every people group in the world so that every person can study the Scriptures and come to know Jesus Christ in their native language. No other religion is so motivated.

This only speaks again to the desire of Christian missionaries and Christian churches worldwide to love and serve under the radar. You don't have to jump through a hundred cultural hoops to come to Jesus. In fact, so far as we are able, we want to bring Jesus *to you*. So in the early centuries of Christianity's existence, this new counter-culture developed where good works were not auspicious, where conversion was not coerced, and where service was not timid.

While the Romans threw their babies away, Christians waited in the gutters and trash heaps to rescue them. While barbarians were forcing "conversions" and violent adherence to pagan customs, Christians were providing faithful and bold witness to the gospel of grace.

This is what has made Christianity so enduring: a completely unparalleled message.

But it doesn't hurt that Christians throughout the centuries have been willing not to kill for the message but to die for it.

Our Chief Strategy Is Dying

It was Tertullian, an early church father, who supposedly said, "The blood of the martyrs is the seed of the church."

What we assume he means is that Christianity has always spread most rapidly under hardship and persecution, and that in fact, the more Christians you try to kill, the more you will inadvertently create. This has proved anecdotally true in places like Asia and Africa, but it would seem that terrorist sects like ISIS and al Qaeda are attempting to circumvent it by literally killing every Christian and presumed Christian they find in their own lands.

But they are not banking on the reality they cannot believe in: that God might in fact be behind the growth of Christianity, that the compelling nature of the Christian religion lies not in its ability to coerce or kill but in the very message of grace, which nobody else in the world has.

Even the clean-scrubbed, polite Mormons who come to my door don't have this message. They are more likely to talk my head off than chop it off, but their message is not much different from that of Islamic terrorists: "make your life like ours or die."

Christianity says, "Give your life to him and live."

The way Christians have proved they believe this throughout the years is by repeatedly lining up to be slaughtered. And Tertullian's dictum lives another day.

We're not trying to win you over with our fancy religion and our behavior modification. We just want you to hear the gospel. And if we must die for you to hear it, we're cool with that. Our dying makes the gospel louder.

Persecuted Romanian pastor Josef Tson recalls:

> During an earlier interrogation at Ploiesti I had told an officer who threatened to kill me, "Sir, let me explain how I see this issue. Your supreme weapon is killing. My supreme weapon is dying. Here is how it works. You know that my sermons on tape have spread all over the country. If you kill me, those sermons will be sprinkled with my blood. Everyone will know I died for my preaching. And everyone who has a tape will pick it up and say, 'I'd better listen again to what this man preached, because he really meant it: he sealed it with his life.' So, sir, my sermons will

speak ten times louder than before. I will actually rejoice in this supreme victory if you kill me."[2]

When the missionaries of other religions are ready to die for their cause, so often they prefer to take others out with them. But Christians are willing to die in order that others might live. And we know that dying is serious business. Dying is a way we show that our lives are not the most precious thing to us. Jesus and making him known are the most precious things to us.

Even the murderous thugs of Isis may figure this out. Their efforts surely communicate the seriousness of their faith. But they also communicate the seriousness of the Christians they murder. Garrett Kell relates the story of one woman converted to Christianity through the horrors of ISIS persecution:

> Salmaa's journey to knowing Jesus was spurred on by emptiness. She lacked peace and longed to know who God was and what purpose He might have for her life. She was raised in a Middle Eastern country where she and everyone around her believed that Allah was the one true god.
>
> But as Salmaa read the Quran, she only found deeper emptiness as she was confronted with a god who was mean, unkind, and unpredictable. After much study, she closed the Quran. She was dissatisfied and left without answers, but the longing to be near to God remained.
>
> By God's grace and wonderful sovereignty, Salmaa was given a Bible and heard the good news about Jesus. She heard that He was not just a prophet, but was God in the

2. Josef Tson, "Thank You for the Beating," *To Every Tribe* (Fall 2009), 5.

flesh who mercifully died and rose to forgive anyone who would believe in Him.

As she read the Bible, she was drawn to the One who seemed to speak through its pages. As she read, she became convinced that the Bible was indeed the "word of Life" that pointed to the "Word of life."

Seeking to know Him came with many obstacles and danger, but Salmaa continued to pursue Him. The longing to have peace, righteousness, and nearness to God could not be quenched. And in recent days, her longing to know Jesus has intensified by the most unlikely of circumstances.

As Salmaa watched the news and saw the murder of 21 Ethiopian Christians by the hands of ISIS, she was strangely drawn to the peace she found on the faces of the men who knelt in honor of Jesus.

How could they be at such peace with God?

How could they look so comforted in their final moments?

Salmaa knew there was a power in them that she did not understand, but knew it must have come from the God she had read of in the Bible—and she wanted to possess that same peace.

Days later, as the testimonies of the families of those martyred brothers emerged, she was once again left baffled. The families offered forgiveness for those who murdered their sons, brothers, and fathers. One mother said she praised God that her son was in heaven now and that she would like to invite the ISIS soldiers into her home so she could tell them more about the Savior her son loved so much.

How could those family members forgive these murders of their sons and husbands and fathers?

This too, she knew, was not a response that could come from natural man, but from God.

She shared that ISIS thinks they are destroying and ending Christianity by killing Christians, but what they do not understand is that their evil acts are causing people to look not at them, but at these who are dying with the peace of Jesus. They are seeing faces of peace, comfort, and power and this is causing them to seek answers, and to come to know the One who is the Way, the Truth, and the Life.

Salmaa's eyes are being opened by the graciousness and mercy of our Lord. And she is not the only one, this is the testimony of many Muslims whom God is drawing to see that Jesus is indeed more than a prophet.[3]

This is why dying is okay. We don't think it is we who make a difference, but God. Nowhere is this more evident than in what Christians believe is actually the power to transform people: not Christians, but Christ. The Christian mission, then, is not really to change hearts—because we can't do that anyway—but instead to share the good news of Jesus. It is the good news of Jesus that actually changes hearts.

Logically speaking, it shouldn't work. It makes no earthly sense. It is not lofty wisdom and it is not a miraculous sign, as far as signs are expected to go. It's really just a message, an announcement. When you break it down—you know, *information-wise*—it's really simply a historical anecdote.

But it's really all we've got.

3. Garrett Kell, "How ISIS Helped Salmaa Become a Christian," *For the Church* (May 14, 2015), http://www.ftc.co/resource-library/blog-entries/how-isis-helped-salmaa-become-a-christian. Reprinted by permission.

See, while some seek to persuade by barbarism or brib-ery, by marauding or manipulation, we've got a message.

Maybe you're shrugging right now.

Some religious missions will put a knife to your throat. In this one, the only throats threatened may be our own. Some crack the metaphorical whip, use the leverage of the law. Us? Anything we might hand out doesn't say "Do this" but "Was done."

What the heck are we thinking?

As Rabshakeh asked Hezekiah, "Do you think that mere words are strategy and power for war?" (2 Kings 18:20).

The answer is yes. Yes, we do.

Because this news of a thing done two thousand years ago is power today straight from another world. It crushes strongholds and destroys spiritual kingdoms. It resurrects the dead and revives the weary. It captures and frees, builds and destroys, transforms and terrifies. The infer-nal prince of the power of the air? "One little word shall fell him."[4]

Some seek wisdom and others seek signs. But we preach Christ crucified. Foolishness. Scandalizing. Where the magnificent gears of religious machinations turn, while the scrolls of philosophy endlessly unfurl, while the cult of spiritual thuggery keeps up its march of bloodshed and tyranny, we sing "Jesus loves me, this I know. For the Bible tells me so."

It's a song for *children*, for God's sake.

4. Martin Luther, "A Mighty Fortress Is Our God," hymn, c. 1529; translated by Frederick H. Hedge, 1853.

And yet in a world of perverse wickedness, of rampant injustice, of deep brokenness, of desperation, and of despair—this one little message is our only hope.

And it is the only power. You cannot stop it. One day every knee and tongue will be compelled to respond to this laughable notion, be it with regret or reverence. "The word of the truth, the gospel . . . has come to you, as indeed in the whole world it is bearing fruit and increasing" (Col. 1:5–6).

10

It's the End of the World As We Know It, and We Feel Fine

HOW THE CHRISTIAN VIEW OF THE END IS JUST THE BEGINNING

He told me his name was Tokar. "Like the song," he said.

"The song?"

"Yeah, you know—'I'm a midnight Tokar.'"

"Ohhh."

This was the first Steve Miller Band–quoting Muslim cab driver I'd ever had the privilege of sharing time with.

I was in a city up north for a pastors' conference and was going to meet some friends after hours at a restaurant downtown. But when Tokar and I arrived, I spent another thirty minutes just sitting in the cab at the curb, talking with my new friend.

How the conversation got started, I don't remember, but it went pretty deep fairly quickly. By the time we'd arrived, he'd already told me he and his wife were waiting for their last child to leave home so they could get a divorce and that he was reading a lot of self-help books.

Tokar's Muslim beliefs were nominal. But he had the same working understanding of life as nearly every other human being in the world: "Do more good than bad."

"Do you want to get divorced?" I asked him.

"No. My wife wants it. She's a very depressed person. I want to help her but she says she doesn't love me anymore and we are better if we are separate. So as soon as our last child goes—*pffft*." He made a gesture with his hand. "She's gone."

"What does your religion say about this?"

"Well, you know what they would say. It isn't right."

"So what do you do?"

"What *can* I do?"

"Love her."

"What do you think I'm doing?"

"Okay, right. I'm sorry."

"Every day," he said, "I just get up, do my thing. Try to stay out of the way. Just try to get through the day."

"That sounds like a terrible way to live."

"Yes."

"What would your religion say about that?"

"About what?"

"Just trying to get through the day."

"I don't know. They'd say it's not good. I should look on the brighter side."

"Look on the brighter side?" That wasn't the kind of thing I would've expected from Islamic theology. It sounded more like Joel Osteen. The more we talked, the more I discovered Tokar's theology was closer to Osteen's than to Islam's. I said, "So when it's all said and done, what happens? When it's all over."

"When it's all over? You go stand before God."

"And you hope he will let you into heaven?"

"Right."

"And how do you know if he will?"

"It's like—" I swear I am not making this up; this is the exact illustration he used, which might as well have been cribbed from someone's fake illustration about sharing the gospel with somebody—"it's like there's a big scale."

I totally knew where he was going with this.

He continued, "And on one side is all your good, and on the other side is all your bad."

"And whichever side is weightiest, that's how you know if you made it."

"Exactly."

I just sort of let that hang there a while. Then I asked him, "Do you think your good outweighs your bad?"

He let *that* hang there a while. Then he softly said, "No."

"I don't think mine does either."

Cynical Optimism

It is Christians who have an optimistic pessimism about human nature. And it's Christians who have a cynical optimism about where the world is going.

The thing that broke my heart about Tokar's story, aside from his acknowledgment that he wasn't good enough to get into heaven but was going to try that route anyway, was his simple statement about "getting through the day." It reminded me of the scene in *The Bucket List* where Jack Nicholson's and Morgan Freeman's dying characters are talking about God on the airplane. Nicholson's character is an atheist and when his friend asks him about his outlook on life, he says, "The wheels on the bus go round and round."

You may think that too. I hope you can see what a depressing way that is to live. But I will admit it's also a very logical way to live, especially if you don't believe there's anything coming after this life.

Christians read the same newspaper headlines that the world does. We see how awful things are. We see the injustice in the world. We see the wars, the racism, the poverty, the epidemics, the depravity.

Like many others, we think things like education and famine relief and debt relief and stronger laws and better leaders can help. But unlike others, we understand that the nations will always be raging in some way until Jesus Christ returns to finish bringing his kingdom to earth.

This is why we are cynically optimistic. We are cynical about human nature and know we are never, by ourselves, going to "figure it out." The problem is *us*. And as long as we are the way we are, we're going to have the same problems. With all the advances in technology and globalization, it almost seems as if we are simply getting faster in and more efficient at exporting them.

When, in Romans 8, Paul says that all creation is groaning for redemption, I totally believe him. The world seems like it is groaning daily. Click on CNN.com. Heck, click on Buzzfeed. Weep for civilization.

And yet Paul says that, contrary to all appearances, creation is groaning not in the throes of death but in the pangs of birth. Creation is not sputtering out but giving way to something. This is how creation ends—not with a bang or a whimper but with a blazing metamorphosis the likes of which we could never imagine.

In that same Revelation vision given to the apostle John, Jesus declares authoritatively, "Behold, I am making all things new" (Rev. 21:5).

My friend Scotty Smith points out that Jesus did not say he is making all new things. No, he is making all things new. There is a redemption coming, a restoration coming, a renewal coming. So what we do here in this life has tremendous resonance. But only if it is done in the name of the one who will be the radiance of the new world (v. 23).

Christians believe that mankind is sinful and thus deserving of an eternity outside the new world that is coming, consigned to the fires and spiritual darkness of condemnation found in the place that is pushed out of the earth by the dawning light of restoration. This makes us cynical about people and the way of people in the world. But we also believe that Jesus Christ has been sent by God to declare the abundant love available to those who will repent of their sin and trust in Jesus. This makes us eternally optimistic, because the old world may be passing away but inwardly it is being renewed day by day.

Some religions look to reincarnation. Others look to disembodied bliss in some place called or similar to heaven. Christians look forward to a forever life in a restored creation, the new Eden made manifest in the world, where there is no pain, death, grief, or lawlessness. We are looking forward to new heavens and a new earth, creation redeemed from the curse of sin and death.

Going to Heaven in a Handbasket

What the Bible teaches about the future was not very well taught to my generation. We heard a lot about going to heaven when we die, but we didn't hear too much about heaven coming to earth.

I know my experience isn't isolated, because almost every person around my age I talk to who grew up in church says the same thing. A friend a few weeks ago said he'd used the phrase "new heavens and new earth" casually in a theological conversation with a fellow church member, and that guy interrupted. "Wait. What?" He'd never heard of it.

This is really unfortunate, because the doctrine of the new heavens and the new earth is amazing. And it's all over the Bible, including the Old Testament where the prophets talk about wolves lying down with lambs (Isa. 11:6) and God's glory covering the entire globe like waters cover the seas (Hab. 2:14). Isaiah is the most direct:

> For behold, I create new heavens
>   and a new earth,
> and the former things shall not be remembered
>   or come into mind. (Isa. 65:17)

The rest of that chapter outlines the beautiful, harmonious quality of that future day of restoration. Even the sufferer Job looks forward to the day when, *even after he dies*, he will nevertheless "in [his] flesh" see God who "will stand upon the earth" (Job 19:25–26).

In the New Testament these prophecies get fleshed out—pardon the pun—to inform us that the resurrected, glorified Jesus Christ will on some future day descend from heaven the same way he ascended, and consummate the kingdom he inaugurated in his first-century ministry.

> But the day of the Lord will come like a thief, and then the heavens will pass away with a roar, and the heavenly bodies will be burned up and dissolved, and the earth and the works that are done on it will be exposed.
>
> Since all these things are thus to be dissolved, what sort of people ought you to be in lives of holiness and godliness, waiting for and hastening the coming of the day of God, because of which the heavens will be set on fire and dissolved, and the heavenly bodies will melt as they burn! But according to his promise we are waiting for new heavens and a new earth in which righteousness dwells. (2 Pet. 3:10–13)

> Then I saw a new heaven and a new earth, for the first heaven and the first earth had passed away, and the sea was no more. And I saw the holy city, new Jerusalem, coming

down out of heaven from God, prepared as a bride adorned for her husband. And I heard a loud voice from the throne saying, "Behold, the dwelling place of God is with man. He will dwell with them, and they will be his people, and God himself will be with them as their God. He will wipe away every tear from their eyes, and death shall be no more, neither shall there be mourning, nor crying, nor pain anymore, for the former things have passed away." (Rev. 21:1–4)

The dwelling place of God is with man, and they will dwell together in the new world. This is something Jesus himself looks forward to in his great teaching on the "end times" in Mark 13 and Matthew 24. He will return and bring both judgment and justice. And he will gather up his followers from every corner of the earth, including those who've departed (1 Cor. 15:35–53) and have been waiting for this moment from their heavenly rest, and we will all celebrate God's glory finally coming to bear on a world that is so broken, so chaotic, so dark in so many places.

Heaven on earth. Can you believe it?

We've all been trying to build it since the fall of mankind; even the irreligious have pitched in trying to find peace and harmony without God on earth, so some deep part in each of us really aches for this. It is the broken image of God inside us that is crying out for restoration and for its soul's match. We will only find that in God when he does this new thing.

Which is why you must not miss out on it.

This is another reason Christianity is unparalleled. There are no alternate entry points. Jesus is the way, the truth, and the life. Nobody gets to this restoration apart from him (Acts 4:12). All roads do lead to the same place—the judgment seat of Christ—and there lies a great fork in the road to the next age. Jesus offers everlasting rest, peace, joy, and wonder in a world that has been redeemed. It's going to be amazing.

We need this optimistic vision of the world, because everywhere we look everything seems to be winding down. *We* are winding down. The older I get, the less messages like "Live your best life now" make sense. And more of my friends are getting sick and more of my friends are dying and, as I said before, nobody gets out alive. Tomorrow is not promised to a single one of us. Your next breath is not promised to you.

What greater hope can the sufferer have? What greater hope can the dying have? What greater hope can those afflicted by injustice or abuse have? Yes, justice against their perpetrator, but then what? The satisfaction of God's justice runs beyond the courtroom and far beyond this life. This life, even if you live to be a hundred, is only a blip on the radar of eternity. One atom in one grain of sand on all the world's beaches.

So many of us live as if that atom's width of lifetime is all there is. We spend all our energy and all our time trying to make this life better. And then it's over. Why not give a little attention, even now, to the endless ages after? There is no greater reality to face.

It was Easter Sunday, 2014, that someone said to my friend Natalie, "Your eyes look yellow." Natalie went to the doctor that Monday, where they did blood work. Tuesday they called and said, "Go to the ER." She was in the hospital for over a week.

They found problems with the bile duct, but in that process also found pancreatic cancer, which, they said, nobody survives. But they also created all kinds of complications in the bile duct procedures that left her feeble and wounded. They talked of air building up, of bile building up, of perforated this and that. And even if those things could be fixed, there was still the cancer, which again, they said, nobody survives.

Natalie refused more treatment at that point. She could not endure any more surgeries. Everything the doctors had done had only created three more things to do. She wasn't going to fool with all that.

She went to a friend's home in Middletown, and hospice took over. They gave her a few days to two weeks to live. She was in a lot of pain. We all hoped the perforations and the air and the bile and all would get sorted out internally, by the body's great design or in God's great miraculous way. But there was still that cancer, untreated. And nobody would survive that.

I read a lot of Scripture to her. She asked for Revelation—with its whores and dragons and plagues and beheadings—and for Ecclesiastes—with its vanities and meaninglessnesses and chasings of the wind. Natalie was never one to shy away from the hard stuff.

I said, "Why Revelation?" as I read Jesus's letters to the churches. "This is what I have against you!" he declares over and over.

She said, "He's not talking to me!"

True enough.

I said, "Why Ecclesiastes?"

She said, "Because I see that having a bunch of possessions and money and fame doesn't do anything. It tells me I didn't waste my life."

Some people told Natalie they were mad at God about her condition. She got mad about their getting mad. "God's the reason we have anything in the first place," she said.

One day she pointed to the collection of cards she'd received. "I almost wish you'd take them all away," she said.

"Why?"

"Because they go on and on about how great I am and how I've done all these wonderful things for them. And they don't know how selfish I am. Anything good I've done wasn't me."

Her kids were all grown. They all came, even her son who lived in Sweden. He said, "Wouldn't it be something if, of all the things the doctors got terribly wrong, it was also this diagnosis about the bile and the air? Maybe, if she starts feeling better, she will change her mind about fighting the cancer."

But, they kept saying, nobody survives pancreatic cancer.

Natalie was upset one day that she didn't know when she was going to go. "They said 'a few days to two weeks' eleven days ago. Now they won't tell me how long I have." She paused, eyes closed. "I guess God knows."

It was extremely difficult watching Natalie, a fit, healthy, thin giant of a woman, shrink down in body and energy. They gave her two weeks.

She lasted nine months.

She was not the first person in my church to suffer greatly under my pastorate. We lost, by my count, five people in a few years to cancer alone. And this was not a big church.

One thing I have learned over the course of our church's afflictions is that when a saint's body gives way, their spirit builds up. They get smaller and God gets bigger, as if their passing is itself a foretaste of the day Christ will put all things in subjection under his feet. And they are not annihilated on that day but redeemed, resurrected, restored. When saints die, we get smaller and God gets bigger, that he might be "all in all" (1 Cor. 15:28).

My friend Richard was in his early thirties when he finally succumbed to the brain tumor he'd been fighting for a few years. He left behind a young wife and two little children. It was brutal to watch him deteriorate, especially for his family, of course. Cancer is not pretty, and you probably know this because it does not discriminate.

The day before Richard died, I stood in his bedroom while he lay on his deathbed. Another bed had been pressed up against it, so his wife could sleep by his side at night. I was told I could speak to him, although Richard was not conscious and was heavily sedated. Because of that other bed parallel to his own, I could not sit near him. I had to actually lie down next to him. So I did.

While his sister and aunt watched, I basically crawled into bed with him, lying on my side to face him, and we lay there, inches from each other, while I looked into his thin face. His eyes were closed and his mouth was open. I could feel and smell his breath, slow and labored, on my own face. I said to him, not even knowing if he could hear me, "Richard, God loves you and approves of you." These were the words the Spirit had spoken to my heart in a moment of extreme emotional frailty ten years ago, when I wanted to take my own life.

"Richard," I continued, "the Lord is proud of you and ready to welcome you because of your faith in him." Then I said something that had been a meaningful exhortation to me ever since my friend Ray Ortlund said it to me over plates of enchiladas at Cancun Mexican Restaurant in Nashville, Tennessee: "You are a mighty man of God."

The words sounded weird given our intimate, vulnerable, tender positions. They sounded weird given that Richard was dying. He certainly didn't look or, I'm sure, *feel* mighty.

In the ordinary, in the mundane, in the boredom. In the throes of suffering, in the pangs and numbness of depression, in the threats to life and safety. Christ is all. And there is more coming.

Richard passed early the next morning. His body finally gave way to the brokenness and the curse. Few people survive brain tumors.

And yet—he did. He really and truly did.

Think of him standing in the presence of God in great glory, presented blameless by virtue of the righteousness of Christ. He was swallowed up into the divine kingdom in which he was already seated with Christ, into the very God in which he was already hidden. Richard was—is—more than a conqueror. Natalie is more than a conqueror. They have gone to heaven in the rickety handbasket of their own bodies but are coming out the other side, into the heaven-swallowed earth, fresh, new, restored, redeemed, *resurrected*.

Jesus looks right into the eyes of Lazarus's sobbing sister and says, "I am the resurrection and the life. Whoever believes in me, though he die, yet shall he live. Do you believe this?"(John 11:25–26).

I do. I really do, by God's grace.

So does Natalie. Nobody survives pancreatic cancer, "they" said. But the blood of Christ speaks a better word. Natalie did survive.

Everyone who is in Christ will survive—prevail, even. Will you?

Three Ways to Live, One Choice to Make

So you have, essentially, three ways to live: by goodness, by badness, or by the gospel. Or, to put it another way: law, license, or Lord.

Some people prefer to live for the moment, to get as much pleasure in as they can, and not think about tomorrow, not think about what comes after they die, not think about God except perhaps to shake their fist at him or his church. Some people deny God by their words, avowing a decided atheism. Some people simply deny God by their life, embracing the functional atheism of living however they please. This is the "bad" or "licentious" way to live, although certainly people who've sold out to it don't think it's bad at all!

Some people prefer to live very religiously, very morally, minding all their ps and qs and keeping a tidy behavioral ledger running. They are doing their best to be good and think good and say good. They serve and give and sacrifice. But they don't love Jesus. They might even go to church, or they might think themselves too good for church. They may be atheists or religious people, but they are trying to "earn their keep" in the world either way, trusting that karma will save them or maybe those great big heavenly scales will tilt their way when it's all said and done.

I think if we're all honest, we will recognize that this isn't likely. A lifetime's worth of good behavior cannot make up for the eternal glory we need to live with God forever.

So there I was in that cab with my friend, the midnight Tokar. He had admitted his good deeds would not outweigh his bad deeds. I admitted the same. He was staring not just into a dreary life of "getting by" but into the unknown eternity, and I had unwittingly exposed his aimlessness. And his hopelessness.

So what do we do? We have three ways we can live, but in the end the first two are really the same. They are both just self-salvation projects, and neither of them works.

But then there's Jesus. He alone offers rest from trying to be good enough. He alone conquers our fears of being too bad. And when we see him clearly—see what love he has for broken sinners, see what hope he offers for wayward travelers, see what rest he provides for weary hearts, see what joy he pours out on parched souls, see what glory he shares with frail human beings—there's only one choice to make. This is what I told Tokar.

In the end, Christianity stands alone, not because it's a "better religion" but because it speaks a better word. Christianity is unparalleled because Jesus Christ is.

Tokar shrugged.

Please don't shrug.

Conclusion

You've probably never heard of him, but there is a fascinating story from religious history about a guy named Sundar Singh. He grew up in a Sikh family in India, raised by parents who sent him to a Christian missionary school so he could learn English. Singh hated the Christians. And when his mother passed away while he was still a child, his hatred for them seemed to grow. (There is one story that says Singh tore a Bible to shreds in front of his friends just to prove how much he defied the Christian religion.)

One day the bitterness and grief grew too much to bear, so Singh went down to some railroad tracks to lie down and die. Providentially, a train never came. But something extraordinary happened. Singh had a "Damascus Road" experience and became convinced that he had met Jesus Christ. He was decidedly converted.

The man who hated Christians became one.

After he converted to Christianity from his family's religion he was immediately disowned and abandoned by everyone he loved. But he'd finally found a joy so overwhelming, he was willing to trade all to walk with Christ. He became a Christian missionary himself, and donning the garb of a traditional Sikh holy man (a sadhu), he went everywhere around his country, telling his own people about the Jesus who forgives sins and redeems brokenness.

Reflecting back on this remarkable conversion, a Hindu professor once asked Singh what it was he had found in Christianity that he had not found in his old religion. This man wanted to know what intellectual point, what doctrinal distinctive, what theological aspect Singh had found so compelling. "Aren't all these religions basically the same?" he asked.

Sundar Singh replied to this professor, "I have found Christ."

"Oh yes, I know," said the interviewer. "But what particular doctrine or principle have you found that you did not have before?"

"The particular thing I have found," Sundar Singh replied, "is Christ."

Doctrine is important. Religion is important. But Christ is supreme. Pastor John Piper preaches that Christ is supreme because:

- He is God's final revelation.
- He is the heir of all things.
- He is the creator of the world.

- He is the radiance of God's glory.
- He is the exact imprint of God's nature.
- He upholds the universe by the Word of his power.
- He made purification for sins.
- He sits at the right hand of the Majesty.
- He is God enthroned forever with the scepter of uprightness.
- He is worshiped by angels.
- His rule will have no end.
- His joy is above all other things in the universe.
- He took on human flesh.
- He was crowned with glory and honor because of his suffering.
- He was the founder of our salvation.
- He was made perfect in all of his obedience by his suffering.
- He destroyed the one who had the power of death.
- He delivered us from the bondage of fear.
- He is a merciful and faithful high priest.
- He made propitiation for sins.
- He is sympathetic because of his own trials.
- He never sinned.
- He offered up loud cries and tears with reverent fear and God heard him.
- He became the source of eternal salvation.
- He holds his priesthood by virtue of an indestructible life.

- He appears in the presence of God on our behalf.
- He will come a second time to save those who are eagerly waiting for him.
- He is the same yesterday, today, and forever.[1]

And this is what I would encourage you to embrace. Not a religion per se, although I have labored here to demonstrate Christianity's unparalleled ideas in the world of religious and philosophical ideology. What I would encourage you to embrace is Jesus Christ as Lord of the universe and Savior of your soul.

I know. It sounds so . . . spiritual. And it is. We Christians really do believe that God's Spirit is real and active and drawing people to believe in Jesus as the crucified and resurrected Son of God. If you are not yet a believer, I hope you feel him drawing you even now.

There is no other salvation than that which is found in Jesus Christ. He is the end-all, be-all.

1. John Piper, "How the Supremacy of Christ Creates Radical Christian Sacrifice: Together for the Gospel Conference, Louisville, KY," *Desiring God* (April 17, 2008), http://www.desiringgod.org/conference-messages/how -the-supremacy-of-christ-creates-radical-christian-sacrifice.

Jared C. Wilson is Director of Content Strategy for Midwestern Baptist Theological Seminary and managing editor of For the Church, Midwestern's new site for gospel-centered resources. He is the author of several books, including *Your Jesus Is Too Safe*, *The Storytelling God*, *The Prodigal Church*, and *Gospel Wakefulness*. His writing has appeared in *Tabletalk*, *Rev!* magazine, Exponential's *Leadership Learnings*, *Pulpit Helps* magazine, and numerous other publications. His blog, *The Gospel-Driven Church*, is hosted by the Gospel Coalition, and he speaks at numerous churches and conferences throughout the year. Wilson lives near Kansas City, Missouri.

LIKE THIS
BOOK?
Consider sharing it with others!

- Share or mention this book on your social media platforms. Use the hashtag **#Unparalleled**.

- Write a book review on your blog or on a retailer site.

- Pick up a copy for friends, family, or strangers— anyone whom you think would enjoy and be challenged by its message.

- Share this message on Twitter or Facebook: "**Read #Unparalleled by @JaredCWilson // @ReadBakerBooks**"

- Recommend this book for your church, workplace, book club, or class.

- Follow Baker Books on social media and tell us what you like.

 Facebook.com/ReadBakerBooks

 @ReadBakerBooks